God at work in small groups

Albert J. Wollen

Scripture Union
130 City Road, London EC1V 2NJ

In association with

The Luis Palau mission to LONDON

Printed by
J. W. Arrowsmith Ltd, Bristol

First published by Regal Books Division, G/L Publications
Glendale, California
This edition published 1983 by Scripture Union,
130 City Road, London EC1V 2NJ
Reprinted 1983, 1985

ISBN 0 86201 138 8

Contents

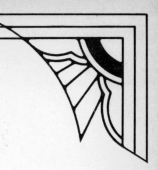

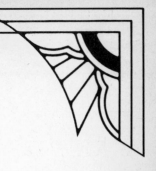

Preface

Although I am the author of this book, I owe its content to the faithful leaders of home Bible classes in Cedar Mill Bible Church. I have not led a class in the past ten years, but I have worked and shared with the class leaders. What I know I learned through them. I am especially grateful to Mr. and Mrs. Jack Boden for the great amount of work involved in coordinating all the classes. Their spirit in Christ has influenced all our activities.

Many have shared in preparing the manuscript. Mr. and Mrs. Joe Bridges worked most of it through its rough form. Gail Denham shared in further editing. My dear wife has spent endless hours typing and retyping the manuscript. Her constant encouragement in a busy schedule helped me to bring it to completion.

This book presents the living and growing concept of a church family. It contains a methodology that has grown out of the spirit of true biblical fellowship and evangelism in the local church. Hopefully it will encourage others to share in the same concept.

Cedar Mill Bible Church
Portland, Oregon

Prologue

HOME BIBLE CLASSES GO BETTER WITHOUT THE PASTOR?

"Ernie, will you lead the class next week? I have to be out of the city."

"I would be glad to, but I can't teach it like you do, Pastor."

"That's okay. Use your imagination and the Spirit will lead you."

That short conversation initiated the lay leadership in home Bible classes in the Cedar Mill Bible Church, Portland, Oregon. The class, which met regularly in a private home, seemed very happy with Ernie's leadership that night, so, I felt free to ask him to take it again shortly thereafter. Over a period of weeks, with the added dimension of Ernie's leadership, the class became so large I suggested we divide to a second home, with Ernie taking a class of his own. It wasn't long before I realized Ernie's class was growing — and mine was dwindling!

7

As a pastor I didn't understand it, but I couldn't help witness something happening in his small group that hadn't happened under my leadership. The Bible was in use, but the "teacher" was missing. Monologue was being replaced with dialogue. Everyone in the class was in the act. I was somewhat fearful what direction this might take, so I suggested to Ernie that we get together as leaders to share what was happening in our classes.

I asked Ernie what he was doing to create such enthusiasm in his class. The excitement was apparent by the fact that he was having a hard time getting the class to close on time! I hadn't had that problem at all.

"Well, Pastor," Ernie explained, "all we do is read the Scriptures, and then we discuss them together."

My first impression of this was of ignorant lay people sitting around sharing their ignorance. I thought to myself, "There can't be much input in a thing like that. They couldn't be accomplishing much. After all, who is keeping them on track? Who is keeping them to the right doctrine? Who is really expounding the text?"

Nobody! But the amazing thing was, the members of Ernie's group were getting very excited about what they were doing. The group continued to grow.

Finally, Ernie said, "There are too many in the class. We have to divide." So I said to Ted, who was in Ernie's group, "You're enjoying the sessions and seem to actively participate, why don't you take half of Ernie's class?"

Ted and Ernie then divided the class, and both groups began to grow. Mine, on the other hand, just didn't. I felt maybe I should stay close to these men and, perhaps, through them invite others in and involve more of the church family.

I made disciples of both Ted and Ernie. I worked closely with them trying to encourage them to share more with the class. But I found they resisted my method. They were having a great time doing exactly what they were doing and were reluctant to do any more sharing themselves. I began to realize

8

that perhaps I should be learning from them. No man, especially a pastor, is ever too old or too educated to learn from others!

I began to realize that the blessing of God was on the lay leadership. It wasn't on *my* leadership. My place was to work with these lay leaders. So, that is what I did. From that time on, I met with these leaders at least once a month. They would tell me what was going on and we would share. I would advise and guide. We'd discuss the problems and each would help the other solve them. Slowly more classes developed and all were under the leadership of interested laymen!

Seven years of time elapsed before I came to the place where I was willing to back off from conducting a home Bible class. During those years I struggled to maintain a relevant place as pastor in the home class.

One thing had gradually become clear to me: the classes functioned better when I was not directly involved in them. When anyone did speak, he seemed to feel obligated to address *me*. Although varying degrees of authority were being exercised by class leaders, it was apparent that discussion was much more free when the pastor wasn't present.

Not until I pulled away from the home classes and stayed at the institutional level where I belonged — working with the lay leaders and giving them the help and leadership they needed — did the home Bible classes begin to really take hold.

As pastor, my place was to meet regularly with the leaders of the classes. I needed to be a good listener. As blessings and problems were shared, I could give some counsel and guidance. When leaders were discouraged, it was my place to encourage and admonish them. Prayer support was needed and I could encourage this in the church family. My reading began to include materials relating to the interaction within small groups. My preaching and teaching began to be influenced by this learning process. To give leadership in the whole church family — that was my role.

9

The Effects of Home Bible Classes

In this early period of the home Bible classes the primary concern was to strengthen the new believers and encourage closer interpersonal relationships. This certainly proved effective. New converts were developing a deep hunger for the Bible. As they read the Bible they began to seek supplementary books that could explain the truths of the Scriptures and help them apply these truths to their lives. Our church library became an important center of church activity. Books were in high demand. New books were added.

As the gap between knowledge and application diminished, concern for one another in the classes assured close personal follow-up. The sense of belonging and being loved grew strong. Openness and honesty removed hypocrisy. Applied Christian principles affected lives all day long, all week long.

For a period of four years we saw consistent growth. Evangelistic outreach into the neighborhood seemed to come quite naturally with the casualness of these classes. Evangelism wasn't something we organized or planned, it just happened. The warm personal atmosphere enabled a stranger to adjust quickly to the group. Masks were taken off — openness and honesty began to prevail. Newcomers were accepted unconditionally. No one was made to feel, "We are in and you are out." Differences of doctrine or theology were never challenged. The Bible was allowed to speak for itself. As one man said after his first visit, "You people talk as though the Bible is an authority and this man Jesus is alive."

How the Groups Were Organized

It became quite apparent that the size of the class had a marked influence on its effectiveness. A group of three couples was usually the most effective grouping. In the small group there was good interaction by all present. As a group grew larger, the interaction diminished. When the group got too large, the leader found he had to carry the conversation most of the time.

The law of group dynamics became apparent: dialogue was effective with groups of seven to twelve; question and answer, from twelve to thirty-five; monologue, with groups of over thirty-five. We settled for the smaller groups of seven to twelve.

Having decided what size the classes should be, we then had to struggle with the problem of how to get the classes to divide when they got too large. At first we tried to break into two groups and go to another house with the second group. The warm friendships that had developed made this very difficult. No one wanted to leave. The leader found it difficult to make the decision as to who should stay and who should leave. The breakdown in dialogue seemed to be less threatening than the dividing of the group. Some classes continued oversized, waiting the dismissal of the classes in the spring of the year.

It was through the experiences of a ladies' class in the morning that we finally stumbled onto the solution: multiple classes conducted in the same home. So, as groups grew larger, they were divided into other classes, all meeting at the same home. Newcomers made up new groups. After a class had been functioning for a period of time as a unit, it was not difficult to move the group to a new host home.

Qualified leaders for all the classes became a problem in the very early stages. The simplest and most frequent solution was that of sharing leadership in the class and discovering qualifications in the group itself. When classes divided, a new leader was left in charge of the older group and the old leader moved with the new group. The new leader would then meet monthly with the other leaders and share his problems.

It was not always possible, however, to find someone in the class who could take over at the time it needed to be divided. This meant bringing in a new leader. We found it necessary, therefore, to recruit new leaders by personal selection from the congregation and from other classes where they were in training. By this method a reserve of leaders could be maintained to step in as classes divided. We used the Sunday evening training hour, the Sunday School class time and, on occasion, a week-night to train leaders.

Some Questions Answered

As time passed, increasing numbers of church members were identified with the home Bible class program. This had a direct effect upon the midweek prayer meeting. Attendance began to fall off. New people coming into the church tended to identify with the home Bible classes rather than with the midweek service. As the problem became more evident, so did the concern of the spiritual leaders of the church. Their concern was two-fold in nature: 1) Was the prayer life of the congregation going to suffer because of its failure to attend midweek prayer meeting? 2) Where could the church family share its prayer requests with one another? There was also a superficial question that arose at this time. What would people think who came to our church and found that we didn't have a strong prayer meeting?

Those attending the home Bible classes soon answered the first question. More people were learning to pray in the home Bible classes than had ever learned to pray in the prayer meetings. The personal concern for one another in the small groups deeply intensified their prayer relationship. Conversational prayer was the most popular form in use.

The second question found its answer in the Sunday morning services. In place of a pastoral prayer, the congregation was invited to share their personal prayer requests. These were written on pieces of paper provided in the pews, passed to the center aisle and collected. Members of the church board collected these prayer requests and came to the front of the church. Each request was read aloud and prayed for. This portion of the morning service was placed entirely in the hands of the laity. Far more requests were shared in this manner, and the entire congregation was involved. After a number of years the midweek prayer meeting was phased out, and a home Bible class began in the parsonage.

As a result of this "community" experience, a marked change has taken place in the whole spirit of our church family. Fellowship, in the true New Testament sense of the word, has gradually permeated the life of our church. Close personal friendships have developed. Genuine concern and care for one another have found many expressions. Every area of life — social, business and personal — has been affected because of these "community" relationships. Although the institutional life of the church remains strong — perhaps stronger than ever — the true spirit of our church is *personal* rather than *organizational*.

The whole experience of small groups has been one of learning and growing for both the pastor and the congregation. The first seven years were marked with problems and difficulties for which solutions came slowly. Some problems have never been solved, because they became too entrenched and habitual in those early years. We had no guidelines for organization because so very few churches or people practiced this particular pattern of Bible study groups. So nearly everything had to be forged out of the metal of experience.

There were losses as well as gains in the process. But through it all patterns finally emerged which were reliable. When these patterns were followed the results were normal and natural. It was not an area that needed a lot of bolstering, promotion or programming. In fact, now that it is properly understood by the congregation, it seems to be self-propagating.

Confirmation of the Holy Spirit's Leading

The home Bible class had been going strong for ten or eleven years when I decided to test it. I wanted to be sure that this movement was of the Spirit and not just the result of an excited pastor who pushed it into existence.

I had been working with the leaders, giving them about six weeks of training every fall, and meeting with them every month throughout the year. This particular fall, I didn't

13

organize any training session. I just let them get back together in their classes. I never met with them a single month from September until March. By that time, many of the leaders were saying to me, "Pastor, what's wrong? You haven't called us together." I made one excuse after another. But what I was really doing was asking myself the question, "Is this really of God — and if it is, will it stand the test of being left alone and still have the mark of God on it?"

By March, I called the leaders together and apologized for what I had done and explained to them why I had taken the procedure I had. The record of the year revealed some interesting facts. We had started the fall with fifteen classes returning from the previous spring. By March we had twenty-five, and I had had absolutely nothing to do with it! So I said to myself, "It has to be of God. To do so well with no pastoral encouragement — it has to be coming from God!"

One of the interesting and exciting by-products of the home Bible classes has been the participation by many members of the congregation in sharing their experiences with home Bible classes of other churches. Hundreds of churches have learned from our experience and are becoming as excited about the program as we are.

I pray that this book will provide a deeper insight into the movement of small group Bible study. God is using this outreach to evangelize, to build His church and to strengthen the body of Christ as its members reach out in love and concern for one another. It happened at Cedar Mill Bible Church. Perhaps God is preparing your heart this very moment to see this happen at your church through the home Bible class.

Part One

SMALL GROUP BIBLE STUDY
IS NO PASSING FAD

Whenever believers have emphasized
open, honest interaction in small groups
as part of their walk with God,
the church has flourished in revival,
zeal and evangelism. Whenever believers have
neglected this small group interaction,
the church has grown cold.

The "small group mentality" is no new thing.
It is rooted in the life and ministry
of Jesus Christ,
the apostles and the early church fathers.

Chapters 1, 2 and 3 describe the pattern
of ministry set by Jesus Christ, the life
that comes when the church
is the church-in-the-home and what
it is like to be the church in community.

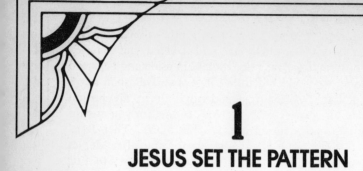

1
JESUS SET THE PATTERN

"Now when Jesus came into the district of Caesarea Philippi, He began asking His disciples, saying, 'Who do people say that the Son of Man is?' And they said, 'Some say John the Baptist; some, Elijah; and others, Jeremiah, or one of the prophets.' He said to them, 'But who do you say that I am?' And Simon Peter answered and said, 'Thou art the Christ, the Son of the living God.' And Jesus answered and said to him, 'Blessed are you, Simon Barjonas, because flesh and blood did not reveal this to you, but My Father who is in heaven. And I also say to you that you are Peter, and upon this rock I will build My church; and the gates of Hades shall not overpower it. I will give you the keys of the kingdom of heaven; and whatever you shall bind on earth shall have been bound in heaven, and whatever you shall loose on earth shall have been loosed in heaven.' Then He warned the disciples that they should tell no one that He was the Christ.

"From that time Jesus Christ began to show His disciples

that He must go to Jerusalem, and suffer many things from the elders and chief priests and scribes, and be killed, and be raised up on the third day. And Peter took Him aside and began to rebuke Him, saying, 'God forbid it, Lord! This shall never happen to You.' But He turned and said to Peter, 'Get behind Me, Satan! You are a stumbling-block to Me; for you are not setting your mind on God's interests, but man's.' Then Jesus said to His disciples, 'If any one wishes to come after Me, let him deny himself, and take up his cross, and follow Me. For whoever wishes to save his life shall lose it; but whoever loses his life for My sake shall find it.'"

Matthew 16:13−25, NASB

In 1965, Dr. Francis Schaeffer made the following comment about the future of the church: "Unless the church changes its forms and gets back to community and sharing of lives personally, the church is done."[1] Many conditions in the church today could have prompted such a statement. But rather than focusing on those, let us look together at a passage of Scripture which will give us a clear biblical basis for what Christ intended the church to be. Matthew 16, which is the basis for this chapter, has something to say about His own personal involvement with the church, who it is that builds the church, the program of the church, and the personnel of the church.

Jesus — God in Person

In this passage, the disciples, through Peter, first personally acknowledged that they understood Jesus' true identity. Peter's words, "Thou art the Christ, the Son of the living God" (Matt. 16:16), are evidence of this realization, which was prompted by the Holy Spirit. Previously Jesus' identity had been verbalized on a spiritual level — by the Father Himself (see Matt. 3:13−17) and by Satanic forces (see Matt. 8:28,29).

Peter's statement, however, is especially important because it shows that he understood the personal nature of God's revelation of Himself to man. And it is this personal revelation that has become the basis on which Christianity stands. Nothing could be more personal than God becoming man to communicate His heart with other men. This is the pattern established by Jesus Christ. Just as the initial revelation of the nature of God came through the person of Jesus Christ, so the ongoing revelation of the nature of God continues today through the person-to-person relationships of believers relating to other human beings.

Jesus' reply to Peter indicates the importance that He Himself placed on this personal understanding of God's revelation. Jesus said He would build His church "upon this rock" — upon this personal revelation of the nature of God. The fact that God revealed Himself in the person of Jesus Christ in a personal way to specific men in history is the foundational rock upon which the church is built.

Jesus — Builder of the Church

Another key point from this passage is that Jesus said, "I will build My church" (Matt. 16:18). Notice that He did not tell His disciples to build His church. He said, "*I* will build My church." And He meant just that. He was saying that He Himself, as a person, would do the work of building the church.

This is why Christianity is so totally different from any other religion on the face of this earth. This is the only faith that demands that the One who founded it, produce it. In every other religion, the founder is dead or will die. Followers may promote the teachings of the founder, but the founder himself is gone. Christianity is unique. It is alive today because a Man came in person and revealed God. He went through the process and agony of death, burial and resurrection in order to personally undertake the work of building His church. Jesus Christ is alive today, building His church.

The Program of the Church

In this passage, Jesus reveals not only the personal nature of the church and the identity of the builder of the church, but He also reveals the program of the church. He does this by telling His disciples that He would need to go to Jerusalem to suffer, be killed, and be raised from the dead on the third day. When Jesus died, was buried, and rose from the grave to be seen by witnesses, He presented the supreme example — the epitome of the role of each person in the church, and of the church corporately, in the world. The program of the church is the death, burial and resurrection *relived* in the spiritual lives of believers, members of Christ's church.

When Jesus began talking about His suffering, death, burial and resurrection, Peter took Him aside and tried to talk Him out of it. Peter had clearly heard Jesus say He would build His church. He had also heard Him talk of suffering and death and resurrection. But verse 22 reveals Peter's disbelief of Jesus' words. Perhaps Peter was thinking, "How can a dead man build His church?" He was using plain human sense.

In verse 23, Jesus sharply rebuked Peter and refused his, or any other alternative plan. Why? Because if Peter had had his way, he would have persuaded Jesus not to become involved in the most personal part of the gospel — that Jesus Himself had to personally suffer and die and be buried in order that those in the world would have forgiveness of sins. The Bible clearly teaches that every man is personally guilty before God because of sin (see Rom. 3:23). Only through the sacrifice of the sinless "Lamb of God" could the penalty for this sin be paid for (see John 1:29). And in order for this to happen, Jesus had to become personally involved with the lives of men dead in sin and to identify with each person. Jesus rebuked Peter for Peter's own good. There was no alternative to God's plan.

The Personnel of the Church

Next, this passage considers the personnel of the church. In verse 24 Christ describes the qualifications of His construction workers as self-denial, commitment and discipleship. "If any one wishes to come after Me, let him deny himself, and take up his cross, and follow Me." Only people who are willing to deny themselves can qualify as the *personnel* of the church.

Do you notice any similarity between the program of the church and the qualifications of its personnel? Self-denial and death speak about the same thing: we must lose our lives and be identified with Christ in His death. Only those who do so will live with Him.

First Peter 1:4 speaks of inheritance in heaven for us. *That* inheritance is actually reserved for the church of Christ. A reserve account is useful, especially when it can be drawn from in time of need. Christ is our "inheritance reserve" in heaven.

How is an inheritance made available? The only way I know of is that someone must die. When a person receives an inheritance, it means that somebody has died and left something behind to be given to a designated person.

Jesus died on the cross, deposited in glory His life, and made it available to the human race. Our spiritual inheritance is directly related to His death. He had to die.

Ephesians 1:18 also reveals another inheritance, this time in terms of Jesus. Paul writes to the Ephesians and to us, telling what Christ's inheritance is. It is in us! Christ died to give us our inheritance, as we saw in 1 Peter. What must happen for Christ to receive *His* inheritance? *We have to die!*

That's right. We must die. This is not talking about physical death, of course. But it is talking about dying to ourselves. The degree to which you and I believe we must lose our lives and identify with Christ in death is the degree to which Jesus gets His reward.

Was there any option for Jesus in terms of Calvary? No! That is why He rebuked Peter. There were no alternatives for Jesus. Do we have any options? Some people seem to think we do. We must realize that we are in the same position that Jesus was: we either die to self or there is no church! Let me say that again. We must have this death-union or there isn't any church of Jesus Christ.

22

Jesus' Life in You

Jesus Himself — the Person — died, was buried and rose again that He might be invited into your human personality to live His life in you and through you. This is the whole message of the church. It is an intensely personal message. It encompasses a person's total self. People sometimes resist talking about this personal nature of the gospel, but this *is* the Christian faith. As a Christian you have nothing else to talk about *but* the person of Jesus, living in you and through you.

Paul said, "For me to live is Christ." This is also why he could say, "To die is gain." The degree to which Paul entered into death with Christ was the degree he could live in relation to Christ.

So many of us try to practice the kind of life that Jesus lived, and fail. Just as the Jews tried to live according to the Ten Commandments and failed, so there are thousands of people in churches today who are trying to live Christian lives by copying Jesus. It can't be done! Surprised? It is hard enough to keep the Ten Commandments even though they may be twisted and stretched a little, but you can't twist Jesus. Don't try. You will be frustrated every morning as you look in the mirror. You must realize that Christ lives *in* believers and guides them through decisions.

Remember, merely imitating Christ's life will never assure you a guiltless, redeemed and victorious life. Jesus rose from the dead, ascended into glory that He might *descend* at Pentecost to take up residence in the body of the church, the believers. His death made life available to us.

If you call yourself a Christian and you haven't seen any change or growth in your life over the last year, you've produced nothing but "wood, hay and stubble" for a year (see 1 Cor. 3:12). It is all waste. Change and maturity are real and visible aspects of a believer's life. Christians who say that they don't want to change are building their lives with "wood, hay and stubble." People may know theology, doctrine and church

23

history and be just as carnal and spiritually dead as those who have never heard the gospel in the first place!

Whatever change or growth does take place in the believer's life is the result of his being willing to have God work in and through his human personality. It is God's intent that we should think His thoughts after Him, feel His feelings and do His will from the heart.

Growing in Groups

What does all this have to do with home Bible classes? The church today is learning to implement and take advantage of the personal closeness in small groups in people's homes, just as the early New Testament churches did. One of the most nurturing and caring environments for healthy Christian growth is in small Bible study groups. We, as believers, must be willing to die to ourselves if we are to grow. When we honestly expose ourselves to what the Bible is saying and lovingly help each other in that exposure, then death to the self-life takes place. In order for this to happen, we have to look honestly at God's Word and see what applies to us.

The Jesus People surprised the established church because they started practicing what they read in the Bible. As Christians, we are supposed to be showing the world we are alive in Christ. But in reality, many of us are living our own selfish lives — doing just what we want to do, but claiming to be Christians. We have not honestly faced the fact that Jesus has given us no option. We must die to self that He might live through us.

Dr. Norman Vincent Peale has said: "The voice of God is no longer being heard in the world through the church. The church is like a big stately tree. It has all the shape and form but it is dead; there is no life; but around the roots of the tree, there are little shoots coming up. These are little groups of people getting in homes where they are being honest with God and to each other, and *there* the voice of God is being heard today!"[2]

24

Do we believe this? Shall we play church or get down to business? Jesus Christ has come to build His own church in us and through us. We are on the threshold of the greatest breakthrough of the church since its rapid expansion in the first century. Lay people are getting stirred up about meeting and sharing together in small groups. They are becoming excited about the Bible. They are being honest and open. They are denying self and discovering that God affirms His will in our personality in a miraculous way. Where people are doing this, God is doing great things! Consider it for yourself, my friend.

Footnotes

1. Dr. Francis Schaeffer, from a message delivered at Forest Home Conference Grounds, Forest Falls, California, 1965.
2. Dr. Norman Vincent Peale, from a television broadcast. Used by permission of Dr. Peale.

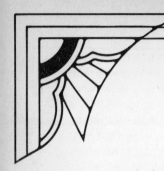

2
THE LIFE OF THE CHURCH IS THE CHURCH-IN-THE-HOME

"And from Miletus he sent to Ephesus and called to him the elders of the church. And when they had come to him, he said to them, 'You yourselves know, from the first day that I set foot in Asia, how I was with you the whole time, serving the Lord with all humility and with tears and with trials which came upon me through the plots of the Jews; how I did not shrink from declaring to you anything that was profitable, and teaching you publicly and from house to house.'"

Acts 20:17–20, *NASB*

From Pentecost to Nero

The apostle Paul, in reviewing the way the church was organized, describes how he ministered to the churches in the early days after Pentecost. He had gathered the elders of Ephesus in Miletus to report to them before he departed for Jerusalem. In his report, Paul reveals two basic ways in which he ministered to these young and vital churches: First, through a public ministry in the byways (*agoras* as the Greek terms it) and second, through a private, more personal ministry in various homes (literally through a "church in a house").

The church was born when the Holy Spirit was poured out and Christ took up His residence in the hearts and lives of the disciples and then of other believers. In those very early days, Peter openly stood in the Temple area and proclaimed the resurrected Christ. There, for the first time in his public ministry, Peter shared Christ as the Anointed of God, the Messiah, the Saviour of mankind, and there 3,000 believers were added to the church.

This public ministry was soon thwarted by the Jewish leaders who forbade Peter to preach in the Temple area. They warned the disciples not to preach in the name of Jesus. However, the disciples went on teaching publicly until Peter was thrown into prison. Then Peter was miraculously released from his cell by an angel of the Lord, who told him to go back to the Temple. When Peter and other disciples went back into the Temple they were apprehended and taken again before the Sanhedrin. Once more the Jewish leaders instructed them not to preach or teach in the name of Jesus, or they would suffer further punishment and imprisonment.

Eventually the disciples were expelled from the Temple area. In fact, they were persecuted so severely in Jerusalem that it was impossible for them to preach publicly even *outside* the Temple. This, of course, was in God's plan, for it compelled the disciples and other believers to scatter beyond the city walls of Jerusalem. They went everywhere, the Scripture says, preaching the gospel.

Wherever the believers went, the one familiar place in nearly every village was the synagogue. It was the place of learning and sharing for Jews and the many thousands of proselytes who had taken the Judaic religion as their own. To these synagogues believers brought news of Jesus' ministry. Paul's early ministry was aided greatly by this familiar contact. The Hebrew language was common in every synagogue, and Paul was welcomed openly as a learned and schooled Jew-brother.

So the ministry of the disciples and apostles moved from the Temple in Jerusalem to the local synagogues. But soon the

Jerusalem Jews who followed the believers wherever they tried to preach and teach interfered in the ministry. These pursuers would persuade the local Jews to resist Paul and the others and to turn against them. If Paul reached the city without announcement, he was able to get into a synagogue and teach the gospel. However, when the opposition had gotten there before him, Paul was not only barred from the synagogue, but sometimes he was beaten by the irate Jewish citizens. We find the later years of Paul's ministry replete with stories of how he was ostracized from the synagogues. Still determined to preach Christ, Paul diverted his interest from the Jews to the Gentile population of a city.

Paul and the other disciples expanded their public ministry by going to the "agora" or marketplace of each community. Wherever people assembled for business or pleasure, there the apostles would proclaim the gospel. Paul delivered his famed sermon on Mars Hill near the marketplace in Athens. He chose to preach the gospel in the streets and marketplace of Corinth, rather than in the Jewish synagogue there. The Scripture records other instances of Paul's preaching in the marketplaces. We know that he preached wherever he could get a hearing.

This public ministry always evoked some kind of response — either positively or negatively — and through it many came to believe in Christ. But there was another form of ministry which seems to have had an even greater impact on the growth of the early church. This was the meeting, teaching and preaching that took place in the homes of believers.

The "house to house" teaching, referred to in Acts 20:20 does not imply that Paul went knocking on doors in a personal door-to-door ministry. Rather, as in Lystra and in Derbe where there were no synagogues, believers met in the privacy of homes. In the letter to the church at Colossae (Col. 4:15), Paul sent greetings to the church at Laodicea which met in the home of Nympha. A church met at the residence of Priscilla and Aquila in Corinth (1 Cor. 16:19).

Each assembly of believers did not form a separate "church" institution apart from the home. Rather, the home was the center and foundation of early church life.

From Nero to Constantine

With Christians being prevented from meeting publicly in Jewish synagogues, the distinction between Christianity and Judaism grew. And thus, the Roman emperor, Nero, noticed and became concerned about the rapid growth of Christianity as a separate entity from Judaism. In A.D. 64 Nero declared Christianity illegal; believers were no longer free to worship. Anyone who attempted to worship the Lord in any public manner, or in any way that could be observed, would be guilty before the law. He could lose his Roman citizenship, lose his property and, in many cases, lose his life.

The Roman decree against Christianity, established by Nero, hung over the church from A.D. 64 until A.D. 313. At no time during these 250 years was it possible for the believers to establish an edifice that they could call a meeting place for teaching and fellowship because Christian assembly was illegal. Nevertheless, the church grew and it flourished! Even though home meetings were risky, group after group was established. Thousands were brought into the faith and brotherhood initiated at Pentecost.

The church, illegal and persecuted, continued to grow in strength and solidarity. That strength and solidarity is vividly represented in an incident which took place in A.D. 170. At that time the Roman emperor wrote and proclaimed that all the Christians in Alexandria were to desist from their faith and meetings or he would send his armies and destroy them. The Bishop of Alexandria reminded the emperor that in order to destroy the Christians over half the city's population would have to be wiped out. (Alexandria was the largest city in Egypt at that time.)

During the first two centuries, when Christians were still active within the church-in-the-house, the church literally

29

conquered the Roman Empire for Christ. By the time of Constantine, in A.D. 300 we can find only one reference to a building which was ever used for a gathering of believers; and that was in Persia in A.D. 265 — not in the Roman Empire. This was the first record of a building being called a "church." Nowhere during that time was there established *anything* like the institutions we know today as a church, but there was a strong sense of brotherhood and fellowship within and between groups.

Constantine, realizing the ridiculousness of the decree established by Nero, not only rescinded that order, but made Christianity the official religion of the Roman Empire. He reasoned, if you can't fight them, you may as well join them! What resulted was a joining of church and state — perhaps the worst tragedy that the church of Jesus Christ could have suffered. It was a marriage between the sacred and the secular — a union of the body of Jesus Christ and the world.

The declaration of Christianity as the religion of Rome encountered little resistance. And many found little difficulty in switching over to the Christian faith. The "climate" was favorable; perhaps because most of those who were not already Christian nevertheless accepted their Christian friends and neighbors. Now, by decree, everyone was a "Christian," whether he was converted spiritually or not!

When the church left the home and became an institution, it died! Let me make it clear — the institution didn't die, the church died. It would seem that with the blessings and encouragement of the government, with the freedom to meet in public buildings, and with the openness and eagerness of the citizens to learn of their new faith, the Christian church would expand further and deeper into the lives of its followers. But that didn't happen.

What happened soon after the declaration of Constantine was a flurry of construction, making the Christian church respected and visible as an official arm of the government. Beautiful buildings were established all over the Roman Empire, now called the Holy Roman Empire, with both the governmental and religious leaders headquartered in Rome. Ironically, we know this period of the flourishing of the public ministry of the church as the "Dark Ages."

When the church became an institution it lost something. As time went on, the church grew stronger as an institution and weaker in its faith. Nearly a thousand years of spiritual, cultural and intellectual darkness over the expanse of Western civilization resulted from a church that lost its way under a powerful politico-religious institution in Rome. (This was after the church had made such splendid strides without the help of *any* institution.)

Now, you might ask, "Are you suggesting that we get rid of the institution?"

No, not at all. I don't believe that the institution is, of itself, the problem. The downfall is that we lost a dimension under institutionalism that needs to be restored to the church. We need to bring the church back to the place where the people within the institution are closely related to one another in fellowship and true community. We must help people find their way back to interaction with each other in terms of their faith and building up their lives personally around the Word of God.

The Church Persecuted but Alive

When the church was under persecution, when it could only meet in little groups, when it was dangerous for believers to meet together, their faith was strong and meaningful, their numbers continued to grow, and in reaching out to their neighbors, they indeed reached across the Roman Empire. That same kind of Christianity is back again in full force on the face of the earth, but not in Western culture. It's in China and Russia.

China is in the same state that the Roman Empire was in before Constantine. It's illegal to be a Christian in China. You

31

can lose your job. You can have your properties confiscated — just by declaring yourself a Christian. But the church of Jesus Christ is growing stronger. In Shanghai alone there are over 3,000 Christians meeting in little groups, not exceeding eight in number. They are studying the Word of God and sharing their faith with each other. Some are even daring to share their faith with their neighbors, facing the possibility of punishment, and even death. There is one man who gives his full time to visiting among these Christians and encouraging them in their faith. Believe me, Christianity is growing stronger, rather than weaker behind the Bamboo Curtain.

We occasionally get a glimpse behind the Iron Curtain. Now and again we see amazing things: folks meeting in little home groups; folks sharing their faith with each other; folks growing stronger in the Christian faith. Because of this close-knit dependence upon one another and their dedication to their faith in Christ, Christianity is growing behind the Iron Curtain as well.

The Church in Revival

It's interesting to trace the history of the church to see what has happened and what influences were present, especially during periods of revival. I have noticed in my study of these movements the presence of one or two factors: the ready access to the Word of God, and the gathering of believers in small, intimate groups. Let me cite a few examples.

We are inclined to think that the Protestant Reformation was brought about by men like Martin Luther, Ulrich Zwingli, John Calvin and others of that caliber. But a close look at this period of history will show you something much more significant — that these two factors helped prepare the way for the Reformation. By the end of the fourteenth century the Bible had been translated from Latin into the vernacular languages of English and German.

As handwritten portions were completed in English, and in German, they were distributed to the people. Few people could obtain all the Scripture because handwritten copies were so costly. But the people were able, even at the lay level, to relate to those portions of Holy Scripture that they did have.

Then another very important event took place. In 1456 the first Bible came off the recently invented printing press. True, the *Gutenberg Bible* was in Latin, but at least it was in multiple print, not the product of pen and ink. It wasn't long before it was distributed among the people. Not long thereafter translations into various languages were begun. Both in England and on the Continent, Bibles were printed in ever-increasing numbers and put into the hands of believers, whether clergy or not. This produced a tremendous ground swell among the lay people where they had access to portions of Holy Scripture.

The clergy had literally locked up the Bible from the common people by way of language; for only a few who could read were able to read Latin. And the Bible was locked up from the people by way of accessibility. As an example, Martin Luther had to read his Latin Bible while it was chained to the pulpit. When Bible portions finally became available, there was great interest. This increasing availability and reading of the Word moved people away from the corruption within the church and into small group meetings in the privacy of their homes. There they read and discussed the Word of God among themselves.

Unfortunately, after the time of Martin Luther and other reformers, churches returned to a strong organizational position. The people again depended upon the institution for their spiritual life and forsook the home ministry. At that time the church went into another very low and dismal period in European and English history. The morals, under the influence of the Industrial Revolution, degraded whole nations to a point where, in the French Revolution, the people experienced a blood bath such as has never been known before — and probably nothing so severe has taken place since. The moral degradation was terrible throughout the whole of Europe. The institution of the church was there, but its influence upon an individual's private life was almost gone.

The Wesleyan Revival

England was in almost the same condition as France and, without question, would have shared her downfall had it not been for two men, John Wesley and George Whitefield. A superficial survey of this spiritual revival in England would credit these men with inspiring the people of England single-handedly. A closer analysis reveals the presence of two factors we spoke of earlier: the Word and small group meetings.

It is true that the Wesley brothers and Whitefield did move up and down the English countryside, calling people back to God. The people who responded met together in what were called societies. In Bristol, Wesley was having difficulty with his Christian society merely being able to raise rent money for the little building in which they met. They struck upon the idea that if they divided the congregation, or society, into groups of twelve, and if one man collected a penny from each of the families, by the end of the week they would have the funds necessary for the rent of the building. So each man responsible for his twelve went from house to house to collect the pennies through the week. He would then bring the pennies to the service on the Lord's day.

As they collected the pennies, these men began to discover some interesting things. Some of the dear brethren weren't living as they ought, and some were abusing their wives and children. In the words of the historians, "Not long after, one of these informed Mr. Wesley that, calling on such a one in his house, he found him quarreling with his wife, another was found in drink. It immediately struck into Mr. Wesley's mind, 'This is the very thing we wanted. The leaders are the persons who may not only receive the contributions, but also watch over the souls of their brethren!'"[1]

Another problem which cropped up in this visitation was the fact that many members were not at home when the lay leader came to call. They might have to return several times before finding the members at home. This was using up too much time for one man.

With these things in mind, Wesley suggested, "Why don't we arrange it differently? Why not have the twelve of each group come to one house and there, together, meet and discuss your personal problems. If someone has a problem in their life that the group can work out together, then you can share these problems at that time. Also you can make the collection on that night and save yourselves going from house to house."[2] This then was the origin and intent of the house meetings set up by Wesley.

When the groups began to meet in this manner they found, to their delight, that a new spiritual dimension was present in the small group that had not appeared in the larger gatherings. So enamored was Wesley with the results of what happened in Bristol that he reported it to the society in London.

The London society decided that they would follow the example set in Bristol and divide into groups of twelve, meeting in homes. Out of this beginning came the Methodist Class Meetings. If you study the Methodist movement and the writings of Wesley, you will find that the Methodist Class Meeting was the bulwark of strength for the ongoing of the Wesleyan revival. These meetings were home Bible study groups — very, very simple in their format, with simple instructions as to how the Word was to be shared and practiced.

Wesley was adamant about the size of his groups. He insisted that no class meeting should ever exceed twelve in number. If it got larger, they had to divide and open another home meeting.

People all over England were drawn under the impact of little groups meeting together in homes, studying their Bibles under the leadership of laymen, not clergy. The influence was so great upon Britain that, instead of suffering a blood-bath revolution as France did, England came out of that period with many wonderful social and moral reforms that affected the whole of their country and much of the world.

The Methodism of England jumped the Atlantic and quickly spread across the United States, not initially as a public ministry, but in the homes as Methodist Class Meetings. The public ministry came afterward, but the home meetings are considered to be the reason the movement spread so quickly and strongly.

The Welsh Revival

We should examine now another period in history just at the turn of the century. This period is known as the Welsh Revival.

During the 1890's, the clergy in and around Melbourne, Australia were very disturbed by the spiritual conditions in the city. They met together for prayer and consultation and decided that what was needed was to get the people together in small groups for prayer just as the pastors were meeting to pray. As a result, home prayer meetings were organized in Melbourne. It was estimated that some 2,000 such meetings took place each week at the peak of this movement.

As the prayer meetings proceeded, the pastors invited R. A. Torrey to come over from America and hold two weeks of evangelistic meetings in the city. Those meetings actually stretched to six weeks. As a result, Melbourne experienced one of the greatest spiritual awakenings ever recorded in their history.

During this time, there was a young woman visiting Australia. After attending the meetings in Melbourne, she returned to her home in Wales. At that time the Christian Endeavor movement was strong in Wales. This woman visited as many of the C.E. groups as she could, sharing the exciting news of revival in Melbourne. She urged the Welsh people to get together in their homes to share in prayer and study the Word. As a result, there began what is now called the Cottage Prayer Meetings of Wales.

However, a dimension was added to the Welsh group meetings that didn't exist in Australia. The people of Wales had recently incorporated music and singing into their worship and prayer meetings, so they sang together as well as shared the Word and prayed. At times, in the height of their excitement, they would get up and go to their neighbor's house and walk around and around it — singing! You can imagine how the neighbor felt. Christians praying for and singing to them. (I don't know what would happen today if you tried it; no doubt the police would be called.)

These Cottage Prayer Meetings laid the groundwork for the noted Welsh evangelist, Evan Roberts. About seventeen months after the prayer movement in the homes of Wales, Evan Roberts began his very successful public ministry. Notice the order in which this took place. The prayer meetings preceded the evangelistic meetings.

So often when we read the history of revivals, it simply points to the great men who preached, as if they were the ones who brought it about. We can begin to see now that that is not altogether historically accurate. Evidence credits the lay movement of the day as the seedbed in which great men found conditions right for revival. And that was evidently true of the Welsh Revival.

The Welsh Revival more totally saturated Wales with evangelical Christianity than did any other revival elsewhere recorded in church history. It even made headlines in papers around the world at the time. A rare and unusual book in my library documents this revival with newspaper accounts both in Wales and England, as well as in America. The Welsh Revival was truly a tremendous spiritual awakening.

The Church Today

Where families are involved in Bible study and prayer with their neighbors, we have phenomenal results. This is true anywhere in the world. Today there is a rising number of small group meetings all over the United States. It's happening inside every church and outside every church.

In retrospect, this may all seem anti-institutional. Far from it. I am simply stating that from its beginning, the church was both public and "house to house." This is the true church in balance. It has its public ministry; it has its house-to-house ministry. There is a need for both — not either/or. I see nothing wrong with the "institutional church," provided the "institutional church" has its people meeting in small groups, interacting with each other, and sharing their lives with each other in the Word — so that when those people come together as a congregation, they have content for that public ministry. This is what I believe church history teaches us.

Looking at our present world situation can be frightening with so many forms of corruption — moral, economic and political. Some say we are heading toward a revolution. That is nonsense. We are *in* a revolution. More has happened in the last five years than in the previous five or ten generations. Alvin Toffler documents this in his book *Future Shock*. We are in the midst of a tremendous revolution!

Where is it going to take us? God only knows. I know one thing: that in the midst of the upheaval of our Western culture, there is a cry in the hearts of people; they want some place to anchor their souls. They don't know where to find it. The church of Jesus Christ is not doing the job. We are losing attendance in our churches rapidly. Attendance in Protestant churches in 1958 was 63 percent of the population. Today's attendance is 40 percent of the population. It is decreasing rapidly every year. Attendance is decreasing more in Roman Catholic churches than in Protestant. But Catholics still have had a far higher percentage of attendance than Protestants. My own state of Oregon has the lowest church attendance in the United States. We're not alone. We all have problems. Where do we go from here?

I was standing at a laundromat a few years ago waiting for some clothes to dry. I was doing this to help my wife, but what I heard that day helped and encouraged me. As I stood there I noticed a couple of women in blue jeans, smoking cigarettes and talking. I didn't pay much attention until I heard one mention the Bible, and my ears instinctively pricked up.

One woman was saying to the other, "We have Bible study

every week in our home," and she told how it had come about. (Apparently, a group of these women had been getting together for coffee once a week.) "We were gabbing one morning when a question came up that we couldn't answer," she continued. "We decided we would most likely find the answer in the Bible. So, I hunted up a Bible, dusted it off, and started searching. We never did find the answer to that question, but we became so interested we decided the following week that we would all bring our Bibles. We did, and this is the second week. We're having a great time reading and finding out what is in the Bible."

Now, these weren't church people at all. They weren't folk who had anything to do with the church. But they had *re*discovered the Book. They were finding it interesting reading.

I have a deep conviction that we are moving into that period of human history when it will not be possible for us to enjoy the liberty and privileges of the present freedom in our institutions. What can survive if our institutional life is threatened? I believe the "church-in-the-home" can survive anything!

Footnotes

1. B. Waugh and T. Mason, *The Works of the Rev. John Wesley, A.M.* Vol. 7 (1832), p. 312.
2. Ibid.

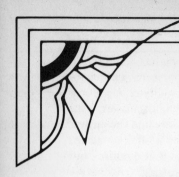

3
WHAT IT'S LIKE TO BE
THE CHURCH IN COMMUNITY

"And the congregation of those who believed were of one heart and soul; and not one of them claimed that anything belonging to him was his own; but all things were common property to them. And with great power the apostles were giving witness to the resurrection of the Lord Jesus, and abundant grace was upon them all. For there was not a needy person among them."

Acts 4:32—34, NASB

For some reason, whenever I send this chapter title to a conference someone feels they must do me the kindness of inserting a word that it seems I've left out. They insist it must be "The Church in *the* Community." That is not the subject at all. The subject is "The Church in Community."

About three years ago the *Oregonian* (Portland's daily newspaper) carried an article about a player with the New York Jets. He had injured his arm and remained in Eugene, Oregon for a number of weeks waiting for it to heal. During his recuperation he came in contact with a group of young couples who were meeting in a home for Christian fellowship.

Upon returning to New York, he approached his manager and said, "I'm going to do a very unorthodox thing and break my contract with the team."

"Now what's the problem?" the manager asked.

"It's not my arm or my health," the athlete explained. "You see, while I was in Eugene I encountered a group of people, and what I discovered through them is so important to me I'll gladly forfeit my income and position on the team to have the privilege of meeting with them."

This player walked away from the glamour of sporting fame to take a secular job and be a part of that little group. It was a close group of Christians who shared their lives personally and intimately with each other as they applied the Word of God in day-by-day interrelationships.

The athlete stayed with that group for a year and a half. He then returned to New York and rejoined the team, but he went back with a new dimension to life and with something to share that he felt he owed to his team. He's playing again for the New York Jets, but he's playing as a Christian with a witness and a ministry to them.

Have you ever thought of what someone like this player, someone of fortune and fame in the world, would find in your church? Would it be something so dynamic, so meaningful, so significant that he would gladly sacrifice fame and fortune in order to be identified with your group?

It is quite obvious that in the early years of the church after Pentecost a unique quality of life was prevalent. People of all walks and stations of life identified with the Christians and were willing to give up everything — and in some cases, their lives — to be identified with them. This was for real.

It's Not Good to Be Alone

When God created man and put him in the Garden of Eden the first statement He ever made concerning man was, "It is not good for the man to be alone" (Gen. 2:18, *NASB*). He was not designed to be a loner. He was not designed for independence. He was designed for family and interdependent relationships.

Sin, which sprang into existence in the Garden of Eden, was in direct opposition to the "community" God intended for His people. God wanted people to be completely dependent on Him so that total community would result. But man, under the influence of sin, decided he did not want God to rule over him. He wanted to play God. He wanted to be independent so that he could do his own thing. Satan's lie to the human race was, "You shall be like God. You can play God yourself; you don't need a God outside of yourself" (see Gen. 3:5). And that spirit of independence is the fundamental, underlying problem of the human race.

Sin breeds the selfishness that causes all the division, both in and out of the church. It is that which caused Cain to cry out, "Am I my brother's keeper?" (Gen. 4:9). That was the mark of Cain, the mark of the degenerate human being. "I don't want to be my brother's keeper," he said, "I don't want to be dependent on him and I don't expect him to be dependent on me." But God expects both.

When God saved Noah, he saved Noah *and his family*. It was a family affair. The ark contained a family. After the time of the flood we come to Abraham. God again blessed the world through a *family* relationship. The tribes of Israel were simply large family relationships.

When we come to the time of Christ we find that the Lord Himself gathered a small group of men around Him and taught them to become completely dependent upon Him and upon each other. For three years He had these men live together, eat together, share together and work together until that togetherness became the very spirit of the church.

After the day of Pentecost we find the church called the "house of God" (1 Tim. 3:15) or the "family of God" (Eph. 3:15, *TLB*). The church is God's family. And the church is the

42

final expression and extension of God in terms of family. It's the purpose of God that we recognize the family spirit of the church. If we miss that we've missed the whole concept of the church. The church was born in community.

We can look outside the church and find the influence of close family life on moral life. Look at Chinatown in San Francisco. Here we find the biggest concentration of Chinese people in the United States. For at least two to three generations they were considered the most disciplined and moral group of people on the continent. San Francisco police used to laughingly say, "If you could keep the Caucasians out of Chinatown, you wouldn't need any police in there." The crime rate was nearly zero.

Recently in Abbotsford, Canada I was sharing the home Bible class concept with a group from some Mennonite Brethren churches there. One of the men shared a story which is very significant to this subject matter.

Katherine, a single woman of about forty, was a resident of one of the labor farms in Siberia. She was of Mennonite background in Russia, and because of her Christian persuasion, she and others of her faith had been transferred to work on a labor farm which was nothing but a slave labor camp. They lived in a disgraceful barracks situation with no central heating, only a board with some straw on it for her bed and inadequate blankets for warmth.

Her relatives in Canada had for several years tried to get permission from the Russian government for Katherine to come and visit them. Finally permission was granted for a three-month visit. Her relatives sent her a ticket and paid all her expenses. When Katherine arrived in Vancouver she was like an "Alice in Wonderland." She just couldn't imagine that people could live with so many possessions. She went from relative to relative in their beautiful homes with their lovely cars and was treated royally.

Of course, the intent was that she would defect from Russia and stay in Canada. After weeks of moving around among her relatives they began to hear her say, "I will be so glad when my visit is over and I can go home." They were puzzled and couldn't figure it out. They had told Katherine that they expected her to stay, that she could find work and would be cared for by her relatives. But about two weeks before the time was up she sat down with her relatives and said, "I want to know for sure; is everything in order for me to return in two weeks?"

"Katherine, you can't be serious," they responded. "You want to go back to those conditions you've told us about with no conveniences of life — just a cubicle with nothing in it? What are you going back to?"

With a very contemplative look, she said, "I don't think I can explain to you why it is I want to go back. All I can say is over here in this country you people have your things and you are busy all day long with your things. Over there we don't have anything, but we have each other. I want to get back to my brothers and sisters in Christ where we live for one another."

Do you know what she is saying? Do you really? I must confess that the kind of life I live has not prepared me to live in barracks just to share my life with people. Katherine was convinced that the most valuable quality on the face of God's earth was the privilege to live in community with her brothers and sisters in Christ, and nothing on God's earth would be exchanged for it.

Community Means Visible Caring

How are we going to develop this kind of community in the local church? How are we going to make the church really feel the sense of family? Can we, with our present structure of the church — Sunday School, morning worship service, committees or evening services? Or how about the midweek prayer meeting (which some call "Family Night") where we try to get all the things rolled up into one package so that we can get them all done with only one evening away from home. I'd like to see one church operating with real community within this structure. I haven't found one yet — not one — where the real quality of community exists fully in interdependence and interrelationship among its people.

In the early years when I ministered with Village Missions and opened small churches on the West Coast, I found that when you had just a few families struggling together to begin a church, they had quality in their relationships with each other. But as the church grew and numbers increased, the largeness diminished this quality until finally quality and sensitivity weren't even expected to exist.

The spirit of the church in community, I believe, is an absolutely necessary dimension to the effectiveness of the ongoing of the gospel of Jesus Christ. When newcomers walk into church on Sunday morning, there ought to be no question in their minds that here are people who know each other and obviously care and are concerned for one another. There should be something that convinces people that the church is God's family on earth. If people who are new in our churches don't walk away with that conviction, I feel we owe it to God to find out why, and remedy the error. If outsiders can't sense the believers' care for each other, it obviously means we are not ministering that quality of life to the people who do attend regularly. We certainly cannot engender in the non-church person the feeling of what we represent as God's family if they see no evidence of it!

What would that evidence have to look like if it were to be convincing? I point you to several instances where I have seen this kind of genuine caring taking place consistently through a local church for several years.

Caring for the Aged

One of the main areas of concern in society today is the care of the aged. With diminishing Social Security checks, relatives who keep their distance and increasing health problems, many aged adults are facing bleak futures indeed. There are elderly

45

people present in every church congregation, and sometimes they are more faithful in church attendance and in prayer than the younger members. How does the church in community reach out to them?

When Grandpa Griffin passed away he was eighty-nine and Grandma Griffin was eight-six years old. She insisted on staying and living in the little house they had shared. A day or two after the funeral, as I was visiting her, I discovered that she just didn't have the responsive memory that goes along with normal living. She couldn't remember if she had prepared breakfast, or who had visited her earlier in the day, or if there was any food on her shelves. I had to go out with her to the kitchen to see what was in the pantry.

Something had to be done. Grandma Griffin couldn't live alone in her little house if her memory was failing her that badly. So at prayer time the next Sunday I voiced that concern and we made it a matter of prayer. Immediately there were volunteers to look in on her the next day and see that she was taken care of. Starting at that time, and for a period of five months, not one single day went by without some member of the church family coming in and spending time with Grandma Griffin. Each day someone prepared a meal for her and checked to see that her house was in order. She was tended to continuously for those five months — and the load was shared by many people. We simply cleared it through the church office so three or four wouldn't show up at one time. Finally, we helped her settle in a nursing home where she was well cared for. But Grandma knew that she was part of the family.

Another member, Ben Day, went into a nursing home. A nurse there commented after three or four months, "You know, ministering to the aged in a nursing home would be the most wonderful thing if all the people were cared for and loved by a church family like this man. He has lots of company and many people showing concern for him and watching over all his needs. But he's the only man in the whole place that gets that kind of attention. In fact, he's the only man I've ever seen

46

who has had all this attention." When God is at work in the local church creating the spirit of community, it's sometimes a source of real amazement to the unchurched and skeptical.

John Sherman, a single fellow who lives alone, was hospitalized. The hospital staff asked, "Who is this dignitary?" It was just explained that he was from a "large family." Isn't that the right answer? One afternoon twenty high school students walked into his room and surrounded his bed. He broke down and cried, completely overwhelmed that they had all come to see him. He was sick for five months and said that he wouldn't trade what happened to him during that time for anything on earth.

"I discovered that I really belonged to a family that cared for me," John joyfully admitted. "The adults, young people — everybody — showered me with their attention, care and affection. It was the most wonderful experience of my life."

Caring for Youth

Youth work has been an emphasis of the church for a long time. Much time and effort goes into planning programs and events that will attract youth to church groups. But what happens when there are youth who are not so easy to love? Here's an example of what the church in community can do about it.

We had a little fourteen-year-old boy in our church family. He was an adopted boy, but I don't know why the family adopted him because he wasn't loved very much. Some said he was retarded, but he was altogether too smart to be retarded. He could "lift" anything from anywhere. He was the craftiest little thief. He had every angle figured out in getting what he wanted from purses, coat pockets and anywhere else.

The natural tendency would be to question: "Why put up with a nuisance like that?" But that didn't happen. The attitude that was adopted was this: "We've got a problem child among us and it is our business to love him out of his problem." The people surrounded that boy with affection and attention, but also with observation. Finally, he found he couldn't move anywhere without someone looking at him. We weren't down on him — just caring. He kept slipping out of the services and turning up in the wrong places. And when caught in the wrong place, someone would put their arm around him, chat with him and say, "Don't you think you should be with the others?"

It took a whole year of affectionately working with that boy. At the end of that year he was so absolutely convinced that everyone in the church loved him — they were giving him so much attention, so much love — that he gave his heart to Christ. He has been living for the Lord ever since. He confessed what he had been doing, tried to rectify it, and enrolled in a Christian boarding school. The first thing he does when he comes back to the area is to "high-tail" it over to the church to reunite with the family.

As a pastor I have found that the pastor's children work against a few more odds than the offspring in other families. There are unwritten standards which they are supposedly compelled to meet. Sometimes if a pastor's son or daughter gets out of line, the congregation looks at that child's father a little askance, as if to say, "He can't keep his own children in line."

We had one son who got out of line. For two years he was quite a problem to his mother and father. But the amazing thing was that not one single member of my congregation ever came to me to criticize my son. I heard them mention our son in their prayers. They invited him into their homes. They gave him special attention. They loved our son back into line — and he came.

After he had resolved this problem and was back home again, I overheard him talking to a friend on the phone, "No, that certainly wasn't the case with me. Nobody in this church ever criticized me or found fault with me. But they sure let me know that they loved me, and that they were praying for me."

I thank God for a church in community. I believe that is

48

how it ought to be. When we love and pray for each other's children, the concern and peer pressure will keep them in line. Several young people have gone astray in our church families, but I haven't found one of them ever being jumped on or criticized for his conduct. Instead, I've seen many of them being given a great deal of extra attention and care. Thank God for a church in community.

Does that happen when someone goes wrong in your church family? Is this the impression that your young people get — that they are really loved and cared for and that nobody is down on them? Unfortunately, there are thousands of young people reared in evangelical circles who aren't with the church any longer because the church wasn't a family — loving, caring and watching over each other.

Caring for Families

We need to keep in mind that the nuclear family itself is the *first* community — Ma, Pa and the kids. What happens when something goes wrong between a husband and wife? I know what happens when the church is in community: that couple is going to get extra attention. They are going to be loved a little more than others. They are going to find themselves surrounded with a group of folk who are concerned and loving and will not criticize. But they will be helpful.

There are a great number of folk in our church who are very, very happy in the Lord because in the midst of their problems and struggles with each other, they were surrounded by a group who worked with them and loved them through that period in their lives. The church family helped bring them back into harmony with each other.

We have what we call the "Deacon's Fund." I don't know how other churches organize this, but in our community if there is any individual family in our larger church family who has a problem, we're ready to move in as a family. We're ready to take over their problems and see them through. And sometimes it runs into the thousands of dollars.

We had a case recently that we worked with, and within three months we had given over $2,000 to that one family. And we kept helping until the family was back on its feet again.

It's tragic that a well-known cult can boast, "We watch over our people, and we provide for them." And yet in the church of Jesus Christ, the church of the living God, if one gets to be a burden we tend to ignore him. Is that any testimony to the world in which we live? In fact, is it any testimony to our churches? We need to rediscover the spirit of community and really care for one another and help each other.

Unfortunately, there are still people in our churches who seem to think that we are in a business; and if it isn't financially profitable we should junk it. If a pastor isn't a profitable asset to the business, they present him with walking papers. A pastor is too often measured in terms of material profit to the institution. That is a tragedy. That is not the church of Jesus Christ. The church is a family. We love each other. We care for each other. We work with one another. And we help each other.

This quality of sharing as the church in community can develop within small groups. Years ago as pastor of a small church, I spent many hours a week in counseling. Now, in a much larger church, I don't spend half that time and I am seeing ten times better results. Why? Because the people are sharing their lives with each other. They are doing the work of ministry among themselves instead of relying on the pastor.

"We Want a Church Where People Love Us"

What steps can the church take to restore community? I know one step that won't work! I can see it now, boldly lettered on the church billboard: "THE CHURCH RESTORED TO COMMUNITY: COME TO CHURCH ON SUNDAY MORNINGS AND HEAR TEN SERMONS ON THE SUBJECT." That's nonsense!

Let me illustrate the fallacy of that approach. A reporter asked a football star in a big Cotton Bowl game this question:

50

"What do you think football is doing for America today?"

The player looked at him and said, "Absolutely nothing."

The amazed newspaper reporter said, "What do you mean?"

"Look down there," the athlete gestured. "There are twenty-two men down on the field desperately in need of rest and 40,000 people up in the stands in desperate need of exercise."

In many churches we see one man in the pulpit yapping his head off and a whole congregation silently sitting still doing nothing. As the *church* in community I think our biggest ministry is to lead the people into small groups where they can share their lives openly, honestly and effectively with each other until we've got the whole church back together as a *family* in community.

Until the church discovers how to be the church in community, to love unconditionally, we will not have the pure movement of the Spirit in our congregation. If we only love certain ones because they measure up to certain standards which are acceptable to us, we are not loving with Christian love. That doesn't come near what God is expecting of His church. We are to love each other as Jesus loves us. Isn't that what He said to the disciples? "A new commandment I give to you, that you love one another, even as I have loved you" (John 13:34, *NASB*). Christ did not love us conditionally; He loved us unconditionally. "God demonstrates His own love toward us, in that while we were yet sinners, Christ died for us" (Rom. 5:8, *NASB*). We are to love each other unconditionally.

If a brother is noted to have some spiritual fault in his life, the Bible says, "Restore such a one in a spirit of gentleness" (Gal. 6:1, *NASB*). Keep in mind that gentleness also involves an attitude of love and humility. If, after you have offered assistance in this manner, and the person does not want to deal with the problem and resents you, the Scripture says, "Take one or two more with you, so that . . . every fact may be confirmed" (Matt. 18:16, *NASB*). If the problem persists, and he still will not face it, the last resort is to call the church leaders and bring the issue before the church (see Matt. 18:17).

We are thankful that only twice during the last twenty-four years at Cedar Mill Church have we had to go to the congregation. In every other case, the problem was solved before it got that far. It was cleared up and lives were set right, or, in one case, the person simply refused to face up to his problem and his conduct did not change. He left before we took it up with the church.

Occasionally someone will come to me or to an elder in the church and tell about a problem in someone else's life. Our immediate response to such a statement is, "What have you done about it with that person?"

If the answer is, "Well, I haven't talked with them," we say, "Go to that person, since God showed you this need, and help that person. Until you have helped that person do not come to me or anybody else." This is the way it is to be handled, and it works.

Occasionally, this spirit of concern alienates some people. We had a couple come to the church from one of the larger churches in Portland. After attending for two Sundays they were called on by a couple from the church. They continued to attend and were put on the church roster because they had been coming six weeks. Then they missed a few Sundays and were visited again. They said, "What gives here? We go to church and you visit us. We understand that. But now we miss a couple of weeks and you come visit us again."

The visitors said, "Yes, every time you are absent from the church for a few weeks someone will check to see why you are missing, because we are concerned. We love you and we want to know why you are absent. If there is sickness we want to help."

They came back a few more times, but then they were missing again. This time I called. They said, "You certainly do watch over us, don't you? Well, we are not coming back to your church. We don't like a church where we are watched like that. We've been accustomed to attend church where no one pays any attention whether we are there or not. We want to be able to go and come as we please."

And I replied, "Well, then please don't come to our church, because we can't have you in our family on that basis. We're a family. We love each other, and we're concerned for each other. If you don't want us to watch over you and care about you, please don't come."

They didn't come for a whole year. Then they showed up again. As they went out the door that Sunday morning and shook my hand, they said, "Pastor, we want a church where people love us and care for us."

No Lonely People
Are we a church in community? Are we concerned for each other? Do we love each other? Will we work to help each other? If the church doesn't get back into community, we will have no church. The home Bible class is one area where this spirit of community can be developed and sponsored, and where people can get close to each other in little groups. Then as they interact year by year with others in the little groups, the area of closeness is enlarged. Pretty soon the whole church family is permeated with the spirit of concern and love one for another. That is the true church of Jesus Christ — the church in community.

Without that we don't know what we are talking about when we say, "Let's have a fellowship supper!" Because many fellowship suppers are simply a group of people sitting around a table, eating food, listening to someone lecture. After it is all over and they go home, there hasn't been one bit of fellowship during the whole evening. That is *not* fellowship! At least, it's not what the Bible is referring to when it talks about fellowship.

It's about time we discovered how to get people together

again so that they really love each other and share their lives with each other and become concerned for each other. There are no lonely people in a church in community. But there is a *world-full* of lonely people in churches where this doesn't exist. May God help us to get back to it.

Part Two

WHAT DIALOGUE
CAN DO FOR THE CHURCH

For too long the church has concentrated
on monologue — communication
going only one way — from the pulpit to the pew.

But churches need dialogue, too!
Dialogue is open,
two-way communication that enables
people to know one another,
to encourage one another,
and to build a climate of trust
that fosters genuine sharing and caring.

People were made to communicate.
The church is people. It is time that dialogue
became the specialty of the church.

In chapters 4-7 you will discover
what dialogue is; you will learn how it works
and see how it can enrich your church
with meaningful interaction that will heal lives
and draw people to Christ.

4
WHAT DIALOGUE IS
AND WHAT IT DOES

Public communication has never been in better condition than it is today. Think of it, we are living in a day and age when communications are so advanced that one can hardly sneeze in China without the world hearing about it fifteen minutes later on TV. The whole world is tied together in a network of communication that is constantly improving. Yet all this highly sophisticated technology has not enhanced the communication between human beings, on a person-to-person, face-to-face level. Rather, in the technologically progressive twentieth century, we are witnessing a disintegration of personal communication that has gradually affected all levels of society and has now even reached into that last sanctuary of personhood, the home. Husbands, wives, parents and children can easily fall into the trap of going about their daily routines without ever really communicating with each other.

The Communications Decline

In a survey taken in the Midwest a few years ago, it was revealed that the average high school student had only seven minutes a week of private attention from his parents! That wasn't counting time when they sat down together and ate a meal, but time they had with the folks. Seven minutes was the average time!

The following scene is typical. You're a parent. You give your child an order for the day as you head off to your respective work and school routines in the morning. "Now listen, Junior, when you get home from school this afternoon, you are to wash the dishes, sweep the basement floor, etc, etc." You give a whole list of assigned tasks to the child. You come home at suppertime; the dishes are still in the sink, the floor isn't swept, and the other tasks haven't been attempted. You ask, "How come?" "I didn't hear you say that, Dad. I thought you said such and such!" And they tell you what they thought you said. Now, of course, you say he wasn't listening. Maybe he wasn't. But whose responsibility was it to see that the information was communicated?

Here's another example. A sergeant tells his platoon one morning, "Men, here are your orders for the day: so and so . . . ." He rattles through them. Then he goes on to another subject. When he is through, do all the men really know what the orders for the day are? Probably not! He gives them motivation by concluding his statement with a reminder that anybody who doesn't follow the orders will be given KP for the week. If a man has missed one part of the order, he'll ask the man next to him or the one across from him. He will use every means to get the full message. He wants that communication badly enough to make it his business to know what the sergeant said.

That type of response is not the usual case in our lives. People just aren't that desperate to know exactly what another is saying. We are not all sergeants and can't expect our listeners to respond with the same eagerness as the soldiers. If we want response, we must get involved in dialogue, where there is feedback and we see that the person with whom we're talking can make a responsible answer and understand what we are communicating.

Society tries to offer its solutions to this problem. Today you can purchase a mail order course advertised to help husbands and wives discover dialogue. It costs $350. Even so, the course has been sold to a great many people. All it does is get the husband and wife together, each with a little pamphlet in front of them to read and practice interaction. That is the whole essence of the course. From this reading and interaction, a husband and wife are supposedly led to a level of discussion, heart searching and honesty with each other. Either they get with it or give it up. It has brought together many a broken home. Why? Because they learned how to dialogue.

The Need for Dialogue in the Church

Sadly, the need for dialogue is also evident in our churches. A preacher has certain problems which entail elements unique to public speaking: faulty P.A. equipment, bad room acoustics, inadequate heating or cooling of the room, glaring lights, or too dim lighting, and even the time of day will affect the effective communication of his message. You know yourself the problem of listening alertly after a late Saturday night out!

Over and above these somewhat mechanical things there is another problem which is common to both writer and speaker. That is, does the receiver get the full and important elements of the message? Let me illustrate.

Most of us pastors don't pay very much attention to what happens when we get through preaching on Sunday morning. We simply say, "There, I delivered my soul. God gave the message, and I hope you heard it!" We shake hands with people at the door, and someone thanks us for some part of the sermon which particularly spoke to him. We're surprised sometimes because to us it was the least important thing in the whole sermon; something that may have been just thrown in on the side. How in the world did they catch that? They missed the message, but caught the throwaways.

There was no way to know this from the pulpit during the critical time of communication. Some "nonverbal" signs do give a certain amount of indication as to the listeners' attention — heads nodding, mouths opening carefully for a stifled yawn, and other little signals. But nothing can really let the speaker or writer know if the important points are being transferred from his mind to the mind of the reader or listener. The only way that we can truly share and communicate concepts is to move from *monologue* to *dialogue*.

Dialogue makes room for necessary feedback, so that out of the feedback, we can evaluate what was really communicated. Until I let you talk with me in some way, I have no real guarantee that you are understanding what I have said.

Pastors, teachers, group leaders, administrators and anyone in the position of communicating the gospel will one day stand before the Lord Jesus Christ and say: "I preached to them, or I spoke to them, and I gave it to them straight." And He is going to say, "What did they understand?"

If I didn't bother to find that out, I won't have an answer. I believe it is my responsibility to know as closely as possible exactly what they thought they heard.

The Function of Dialogue

Three purposes help us to clarify the function and definition of dialogue.

The *first* purpose is to allow persons to interrelate with each other. As they interrelate, they discover the truth about each other, they have opportunity not just to speak, but to share with each other, and they are able to get feedback on what they have said. In short, dialogue enables people to talk things out.

Until you can be perfectly honest and open with another person, and share what is on your heart — back and forth in dialogue — you won't know how to handle new ideas or

61

beliefs different from yours without being threatened by them. You'll be defensive until you learn to dialogue. Many preachers who are dedicated and sound theologians are stuck with the same problem themselves. They can't accept criticism. They are defensive creatures. They may win arguments, but they lose all their friends.

Until we learn how to dialogue with each other, we won't know how to get right with God. Even our *concept* of God may be warped and twisted. We hear about God from the pulpit; we read about God from literature and the Bible, but it would amaze you to learn what even dedicated Christians have as a concept of God. If you sat down with your congregation or a group of Christians and gave them a test with a series of questions on what God means to them — in terms of definition — you might be very surprised to learn what sort of a God your people are worshiping. It might not be totally biblical. However, it could be we haven't dialogued enough to discover what they really envision when they use the word "God" in their vocabulary.

Secondly, dialogue helps us understand what another person believes as we help him make "yes" or "no" decisions responsibly. As a pastor, I am confronting my congregation with the most profound responsibility in human existence. And that can be expanded to preachers throughout the world. We are asking them to say "yes" or "no" to facts which will affect their eternal destiny!

In fact, we are often asking people to respond to the gospel without giving them an accurate understanding of what that response really entails. It is a pity. We lead people to the point of self-evaluation. We press for a decision. Do we really know what a person believes in making that decision? Too often we do not. Too often, when someone comes forward in a church service, he is highly emotional about what has just taken place. He is making a decision in terms of the sermon's emotional content. Perhaps we haven't given him time to discover what he really thinks that decision means. He makes the decision then goes away, and to our chagrin he later turns away from God. We thought he was "turned on" for God, and perhaps he was at first. We wonder why he made a decision, but didn't go on? What decision did he *actually* make?

I've traced some of these decisions from my earlier ministry, wondering what the real response was when I got people to come forward. One fellow said to me, "Well preacher, you'd been naggin' me and fussin' at me for so long, both in the services and every time you met me, that I decided if I went foward you'd get off my back!"

He made a decision — to get me off his back. I didn't know that my nagging was the framework and motivation for his decision. How firm can such a decision be? You see, the purpose of dialogue is to interrelate so that you have given a proper framework in which a decision of "yes" or "no" is meaningful — not made for spite or personal reasons.

The *third* purpose of dialogue is to restore the tension between vitality and form. We usually don't have any problem with the form. We've really got that. There is nothing wrong with the basic form of the church of Jesus Christ. It's been tried, tested and proved. It has come out of years of historical reality and is not something we have conjured up recently. But much can be said about the vitality in that form. Many people sitting in the framework of our church activities are not finding any vital, dynamic life-changing force in the form. And we had better find out why they aren't finding it.

If we are going to achieve vitality in the form of our church services, our church activities, our young people's meeting, our church outreach, our visitation programs — anything that we are doing as a church — we must find out through feedback what is really happening. Get the people to interact with each other, to discover whether the church is alive or not, and through this dialogue, find life.

Perhaps you have heard about the Peninsula Bible Church in California, where the pastor, Ray Stedman, conducts "Body Life" services on Sunday evenings. Because the church

63

is located near five colleges, it has had a tremendous ministry on the campuses and a great influence with the young people. These young people in small groups interacting with their leaders, have been wide open to share their hearts with each other in true dialogue.

One Sunday night, the church dared to invite these young people to interact among themselves in the evening service as they had been doing in their little groups. They simply opened their hearts to each other in the presence of the adults in the congregation. It wasn't a large congregation on that first night, about 300.

The interaction began with the pastor himself sharing something very honestly from his own soul. Then the kids began to get honest with each other. They prayed for each other. They shared and then prayed for each other again. Talked some more and prayed some more — interacting with each other.

The adults discovered that here was a spirit of community, a spirit of love and honesty and openness that they had never seen in the church before. They began longing to have among themselves the kind of relationship they saw in the young people. Pretty soon it moved from the young people to the adults.

When the whole church got involved, everyone wanted to come and see a church body where the members were sharing their lives with each other. Until finally the auditorium that seats 1,100 had people standing along the walls during those Sunday night services.

Do you see what dialogue can mean to a body of believers? Solid and meaningful spiritual growth!

5

THE EARLY CHRISTIANS KNEW HOW TO DIALOGUE

In the history of mankind there have been many great teachers — men whose names have been revered because of their ability to share truth and to pass it on to others. But none come near the teaching prowess of Jesus Christ.

During Jesus' teaching ministry He chose twelve men with whom He shared every aspect of His life. He ate with them. He slept among them. He conversed with them. He shared everything on a personal and intimate basis. The element of dialogue played a very important part in the training of these disciples.

Dialogue in the Ministry of Christ

Sometimes Christ used lecture when He addressed the disciples. On other occasions, they sat with Christ and probed deeply, searching and seeking into the meaning of what He had been sharing with them. Sometimes they made it very plain that they did not understand what He had said, as in the case of Thomas when he asked, "Lord, we don't know where you are going, so how can we know the way?" (John 14:5, *NIV*).

At other times Christ, in response to their questioning and searching, spoke so plainly that they answered, "Now you are speaking clearly and without figures of speech" (John 16:29, *NIV*). Whenever He was in dialogue with His disciples, Christ deliberately drew out their reactions and responses to what they had seen and were being taught. Thus He modeled the kind of dialogue where honest communication and learning can take place.

One of the best illustrations of this occurred when He inquired of His disciples, "Who do men say that I am?" (see Matt. 16:13). After their initial response, He asked the deeper question, "But who do you say that I am?" (see Matt. 16:15). Note the very significant response from Peter, "Thou art the Christ, the Son of the living God" (Matt. 16:16). By initiating this dialogue, Christ gave the disciples an opportunity to express what they were thinking at a deep and honest level.

Emotions in Dialogue

These examples from Scripture show that dialogue involves much more than intellectual communication with other people. True dialogue also demands communication and understanding at the emotional level.

For instance, when he dialogued with the woman at the well, Jesus probed gently, but deeply and personally into the woman's life, until finally, in utter embarrassment, she tried to change the subject. This was because she did not want to discuss the threatening issues of her personal life. She felt it much safer to keep the conversation on theological issues, which were less threatening to her. But Jesus would not be deterred. He returned again to the woman's inner need, disclosing that, like everyone else, she had a sin problem she could not solve. By getting past the theological issues to the personal issues, Jesus confronted her with the empty reality of her own life at the *emotional* level. Only when she had been led to dialogue at the level of her emotions, where she really lived, did she recognize who He was. And only then could she change (see John 4:5—29).

Many of the interactions between Jesus and His disciples reveal displays of anger, fear, love and courage. The night of the Last Supper was charged with emotion. The disciples argued among themselves as to who was the greatest, and Jesus talked to them about servanthood (see Luke 22:24—27). That was emotional dialogue. When Jesus revealed that one of His trusted band of men was going to betray Him, each of them anxiously questioned Him as to whether he was the one (see Mark 14:17—19). By doing so, each of them admitted honestly that he knew he was capable of denying Jesus. That was honest dialogue. Peter vehemently asserted that he would never leave Jesus, but would willingly die with Him (see John 13:37,38). Jesus responded by telling Peter he would deny Him three times. Again, that was honest, emotional dialogue.

In these dialogues, there was no place for phoniness or trying to cover up feelings. In the presence of Jesus, the disciples could only respond by reflecting what they were honestly feeling inside. When they displayed feelings that were wrong, Jesus corrected them. When their feelings were right, Jesus affirmed them. Through this honest dialogue, which could not have happened if they had kept their feelings bottled up inside, the disciples experienced change and growth and the freedom to be themselves.

Dialogue in the Ministry of Paul

The whole process of dialogue, as practiced by Jesus Christ with the Twelve, became the basis upon which the future church was to develop its ministry. Deep personal involvement and the intimate sharing of their lives became a major characteristic of the disciples' ministry. This pattern is exemplified in the life of Paul.

We find Paul always in the company of several others. He

was never a loner. He never carried the truth of the gospel merely as a private lecturer. He always brought a band of men with him so that the establishment of the truth was presented in the framework of a group and human personality.

The rabbinical training Paul received in his childhood, and the advanced training from the school of Gamaliel, powerfully influenced his method for sharing the gospel. It was the custom of the Jews not merely to state facts but to reason and discuss back and forth, spending hours in dialogue in search of truth. Acts 17:17 implies that this typically Jewish manner of reasoning and sharing developed between Paul and those with whom he invested himself. The Greek word, *dialectus,* has all the basic meanings of our English word, "dialogue." Paul continuously used this method of reasoning, persuading and sharing, in order to get the truth of the gospel across.

Dialogue as Seen in John's Letters

In his first Epistle John uses every conceivable phrase and word that will imply a close, intimate, personal involvement with Jesus Christ. "That . . . which we have heard, which we have seen with our eyes which we have looked upon, and our hands have handled . . ." (1 John 1:1) — everything in this language implies that relationships among Christians are to be intimate and personal.

John had discovered the true personality of God through the continued encounter with Christ. He had shared Christ's deepest thoughts, His inner emotions, His attitudes and actions in life. He wanted to share this experience with other believers. This quality of relationship was conveyed in his words. "We proclaim to you what we have seen and heard, so that you also may have fellowship with us" (1 John 1:3, *NIV*).

John would have us to understand that Christian *koinonia,* or fellowship, is not simply the exchange of philosophical thought, not simply the stating of a doctrinal truth, but rather the intimacy of personal involvement and the heart-to-heart contact.

When John speaks of eternal life, he is speaking of a quality of life relationship here on earth right now. "If we walk in the light, as he is in the light, we have fellowship [right now] one with another" (1 John 1:7). John demands an open, honest, unreserved relationship with Jesus Christ and with one another as believers.

The warm, emotional terminology used by John throughout his letter implies the deep, human relationship initiated by Christ and established in Christian fellowship.

The purpose of his writing the letter was that Christians might experience life-transforming power with Jesus Christ — power which can permeate the depths and feelings of their personal lives. Such a quality of life can only be learned and experienced by long periods of dialogue between personalities. It's this dialogical process that constitutes the true essence of Christian life.

Dialogue in the Church Family

One response of the early believers to the message of salvation was personal concern for one another. Acts 2 tells us that those who had extra belongings sold what they had and brought the proceeds to share with others. Deacons were appointed to see that all the members of the church family were properly cared for.

The early believers also recognized that theirs was a family relationship. The older men were called fathers, the younger men and women were brothers and sisters. The older women were treated as mothers. Widows were to be given special recognition and cared for within the family framework. A strong rebuke was given to church families who did not care for their own.

If this, then, is the true spirit of the church — that we are to be as a big family sharing in a close personal, intimate relationship — it is hardly conceivable that the church could so function within the present framework of a ministry based on monologue! Unless we have a place for dialogue — the opportunity to really get intimately acquainted with one another — we can hardly expect the New Testament spirit of *family* to pervade in the present church structure.

Dialogue in the Body of Christ

The church is also likened to the human body, with its multiple members and functions operating in relationship to one another, so as to have total interdependence. Each part of the body of Christ is to share its special gift with other parts, thereby giving the body its health and strength. The body is considered to be healthy only when each one of these members can minister to one another, exercising the gifts with which they are endowed by the Holy Spirit. Without personal involvement, one can hardly see the fulfillment of all that is implied by the church, the body of Christ. Until the members of any local church can share burdens, concern, deeper personal yearnings and problems with one another, they cannot expect to fulfill their responsibilities as parts of the body of Christ.

Dialogue and Reconciliation

The fundamental message of the church, both to itself and to the world, is reconciliation — reconciliation to God and reconciliation to one another. The message of the church can only be understood in the world and interpreted to the world when the world sees Christians demonstrating a growing and intensified relationship of reconciliation.

It has become increasingly more difficult for the world to understand the message of reconciliation when it sees the members of the church body coming to assemblies and disbanding from these assemblies with no closer relationship to one another than before they came. Many church members attend services with regularity, responding to each other with no more than a casual nod and recognition of faces. Tragically, there is often more personal communication and sharing in the local tavern over a glass of beer than there is in the professed fellowship of the body of Christ over coffee and donuts!

When Christians get back into dialogue with each other and when there develops deep personal sharing — only then can the world be impressed with our message of reconciliation. Dialogue is *essential* to a true expression of the church as it seeks to reach the world round about us.

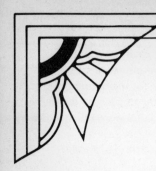

6
LOVE, HONESTY, TRUST, UNITY — THE ELEMENTS OF DIALOGUE

Paul concludes 1 Corinthians 13 with reference to faith, hope and love — a trilogy of qualities essential to Christian living. Dialogue also has its trilogy of essential elements — trust, honesty and love. As with Paul's trilogy, so also with the dialogue trilogy, love is the greatest.

The Element of Love

Reuel Howe, author of the book, *The Miracle of Dialogue*,[1] has stated that dialogue is to love as blood is to the body. As blood provides the elements to build the human body, so love shared in dialogue brings the life-giving force to build the body of Christ.

Here is how this principle worked out in the life of one of

72

our members. When Bob first began attending a home Bible class, he had no idea what effect it was to have upon his life. He had grown up in the church and had taken it for granted as many others do. He attended with a degree of regularity. He was not averse to doing his share by accepting some responsibility in the church's activity. He was serving as an elder at the time he first began attending a home Bible class. He had no deep interest in the study of the Bible. His prayer life was very casual. Life had made no unusual demands and there was no point of crisis in his spiritual experience. Bob aptly described himself as a "Sanka" Christian, where 95 percent of the spiritual ingredients were missing!

Bob hadn't attended the Bible class long before he became aware of the genuine love and concern for one another among members of the group, and he began to experience it himself. They were probing for the real meaning of their Christian faith and its expression in love to each other. A whole new concept of Christian truth began to dawn upon Bob. The Bible became a living book. Its teachings had a direct relationship to everyday life.

In the warmth of sharing, God began to apply these truths to Bob's daily life. Soon he found himself sharing what he was learning and experiencing with others. This developed into a concern to take a more active part in making Christ known.

Bob accepted the responsibility of being a leader in a Bible class. Such a hunger for the Bible developed that he began to do considerable study in addition to meeting with the class. Prayer took on new meaning. Talking with God became a part of his everyday life and thought. His Christian life was shared with those with whom he worked. He joined the Gideons and took an active part in their preaching ministry. He has grown into a spiritual leader, loved and revered by all who know him.

Love Heals

God not only builds the body, He also brings healing to the parts of the body that are ill. So love, shared in dialogue, is the healing force in the lives of those who are in a small group.

Jean began attending a home Bible class because it was in her mother's home. She considered herself an agnostic. At the same time she was living with a divorced man named Mark. At first she was politely tolerant of the group. As time went on, however, she sensed a spirit of love and openness that intrigued her. The Bible was read and shared on its face value. No one placed their private interpretation upon it, nor did they sit in censure of one another.

Gradually, Jean began to consider Jesus in an entirely different light. She was encountering Him as a person in the lives of the members of the class as they, in turn, shared Christ in their daily experiences. She was neither censured nor reprimanded by any because of her conduct. She then persuaded Mark to join her in the class. Soon they felt they needed to be married and so they were.

Jean was the first to recognize Christ as her Saviour, and Mark saw his need for Christ soon after. The healing in their lives was obvious to everyone. They began sharing their faith with those about them and making every effort to develop their lives in a spiritual atmosphere. They began attending church services regularly and taking in every form of training that was made available to them in the church. A deep sense of guilt that had disturbed Jean soon found relief in the love and fellowship of other Christians.

Love Brings Vitality

As blood provides the body with the energy for service, so love gives the vitality to the believer for Christian service. June had always considered herself a good, loyal church member from her youth. She could play the piano and organ, and on occasion served the church in this area. As a growing family demanded more and more of her time, she felt less and less free to serve outside of their home. When she began attending home Bible classes her life took on new dimensions.

June began to open up and share freely in the warm, loving

atmosphere of the class. She found herself assuming the role of a sister in a big family. As the class grew, June accepted leadership. The excitement of Christian growth led her to explore books, and she became an avid reader of good Christian literature. This, in turn, led her to develop a library in her church. She was not satisfied with just a good collection of books, but learned and demonstrated ways to make the library in the local church one of the most effective libraries in the community.

The library ministry led June to another area of service. She saw the usefulness of Christian tapes and began collecting them to be shared with fellow believers. In time the tape ministry became so effective and so widespread that she trained someone else for the library and concentrated on the tapes.

June continued her leadership in home Bible classes. Out of this developed an opportunity to share her experiences in a home Bible class panel, visiting in other churches. She became an effective speaker and began to be used in an ever-widening circle to minister to others. Her continued involvement as a leader in home Bible classes gave her an increased popularity with her neighbors who were continually calling her by telephone and sharing their problems.

June never neglected her family, nor did they ever feel left out because of her services. The disciplines in her life enhanced her place as a mother and wife and gained the respect and joy of all her family. The loving relationship of all her church family has found its full expression in a vital Christian service.

The Element of Honesty

To effectively share love, people must accept one another with nonjudgmental attitudes. God's love is unconditional. We may not agree with another's behavior, but we can love him as a person. A willingness to know a person as he is often opens the door of understanding and eventually can bring about changes in action. This leads to the second element in dialogue, that of open honesty. Open honesty is simply the willing exposure of one's personality.

To a greater or lesser degree everyone playacts in life. Very early in life we learn how to impress one another by adopting certain actions, mannerisms and expressions. We put on the mask that suits the occasion. We become adept at impressing people to get what we hope is a favorable response. With some people this playacting dominates their personality. There may be a variety of reasons for the development of this camouflage, but basically it is caused by deep insecurity and fear of judgment or rejection. Christian love shared in a small group through dialogue, provides a safe environment for lowering and removing these masks.

One man who seldom shared in conversation, other than by cracking jokes, confessed he was afraid to be serious because he wasn't too well educated. But when he found he was fully accepted in the group he entered freely into the discussion.

There are occasions when open honesty is dramatic in a small group. Ruth had been coming only a short time to a ladies' group when she shared a secret. Inasmuch as this has been shared publicly by Ruth and her husband, I'll let the class leader tell it as it occurred.

"Ruth was new to our Tuesday morning Bible study and all the girls warmly welcomed her. We were a very sincere and expressive group which had developed an openness. Ruth felt this openness and blurted out, 'My husband is an alcoholic.' Then covering her face she sighed deeply and said, 'Oh, I have never told anybody about this, and I don't want to betray my husband's confidence.' Many of the girls reassured her that this would not be talked about outside our group, but that it would be made a matter of prayer.

"To our astonishment, Alice spoke up, 'I know what you are saying, because my husband is an alcoholic also. But God has been showing me that I have been the reason he has become an alcoholic. Maybe you should ask God to show you if you are the problem.'

76

"You could have heard a pin drop. There was that quietness that you feel. No one knew what to say. Then someone prayed. We dismissed and went home.

"Ruth was prayed for much that week. We didn't know if she would have the courage to return. But, praise the Lord, she did and with great openness told us how she had examined herself and God did reveal that she was a nagging wife. She said, 'We had two days of calm because I shut up, and he didn't need drink to turn me off.' Praise the Lord.

"Ruth continued coming and within the next couple of weeks gave her heart to the Lord. After a few months her husband went to the pastor because as he put it, 'My wife's life has so changed, I want what she has. Our home now is a place where I love to be.' As he left the office that day he too was a 'new creature in Christ Jesus, old things were passing away and all things were becoming new.'"

The Element of Trust

The element of trust is fundamental to dialogue. Without trust, group encounter can be no more than game playing. Trust cannot be forced or assumed, it must be developed with time and patience. Like a gentle dove it is sensitive and may be frightened off. Trust has varying degrees of depth. It may linger at a shallow level until some sharing experiences prove the reliability of the group. A deep crisis lovingly shared may move it to greater depths.

The leader in a group must furnish the basis for a growing trust. No one should be forced to share, but everyone should be carefully encouraged to do so. When people feel that they are being forced to trust, they become defensive. Then barriers are built up and sometimes people stay away. One man who had attended a group for several months had learned to share quite freely. But no one noticed that he had never volunteered to read. Then one evening the leader asked him to read. He made some excuse about his eyes and refused. He never returned to class again.

The Element of Unity

When a group of people share together over a period of time using the Bible as the basis of that relationship, there should occur some resemblance to Acts 2:1. The disciples had been together over a period of ten days. By that time, "they were all with one accord."

The element of unity in dialogue may not be evident in the beginning, but if the other elements are present, one of the results will be unity. Unity is something of a thermometer that measures the spiritual temperature of the group.

It is apparent by now that the elements of dialogue are more in the area of emotion than intellect. Intellectually understanding all these elements of dialogue will not produce dialogue. True dialogue must take place at the emotional level. This is not to say that the intellect is not needed in dialogue. On the contrary, the greater the emotional freedom, the more that can be shared intellectually.

Emotional hang-ups are the chief barriers to learning. People really aren't listening when they are bottled up emotionally. Or it may be they heard the words but twisted and warped them because of emotional barriers.

The dialogical person has a great deal of emotional freedom. He is as capable of listening as of talking, he is sensitive to the feelings of others but not threatened by them. This behavior does not produce judgment but rather interest and concern to understand and share. Life can be a great adventure discovering people in all walks of life. In a spirit of Christian love we have something to learn from everyone and, hopefully, something tremendous to share from Jesus Christ.

The following poem is an excellent illustration of what can happen when all the elements of dialogue are working in harmony.

THAT'S MY SOUL

"That's my soul lying there.

You don't know what a soul is?
You think it's some kind of ghostly sheetlike thing you can
    see through and it floats in the air.
That's my soul lying there.

Remember when my hand shook because I was nervous in the
    group?
Remember the night I goofed and argued too much and got
    mad and couldn't get out of the whole mess?
I was putting my soul on the line.

Another time I said that someone once told me something
    about herself that she didn't have to.
I said that she told me something that could have hurt her.
And I guess I was asking you to do the same.
I was asking you to let me know you.
That's part of my soul too.

When I told you that my mother didn't love my dad and I
    knew it as a kid,
When I said that my eyes water when I get hurt even though
    I'm thirty-four and too much a man to cry.
I was putting my soul out there in the space between me and
    you.
Yeah, that's my soul out there.

I've never met God.
I mean that I've never met the old man that sits on a cloud
    with a crown and a staff and knows everything and is
    everything and controls everything.
But I've met you.

Is that God in your face?
Is that God in your soul lying there?

Well, that's my soul lying there.
I'll let you pick it up.
That's why I put it there.

It'll bruise and turn rancid like an old banana if you want to
    manhandle it.
It'll go away if you ignore it.

But if you want to put your soul out there beside it, there may
    be love.
There may even be God."[2]

— by Ernest L. Stech

Footnotes

1. Reuel L. Howe, *The Miracle of Dialogue* (New York: Seabury, 1963).
2. Ernest L. Stech, "That's My Soul." Quoted by Bruce Larson in *No Longer Strangers*
   (Waco, Texas: Word Books, 1971) pp. 35, 36.

7

WHAT HAPPENS
WHEN PEOPLE DIALOGUE
– SOME CASE STUDIES

When Jack came to the home Bible class in Bob's home, he really didn't know what he was getting into. His wife, Mary, had been attending a morning ladies' class and was very enthusiastic about it. This was an evening class for couples. He was attending the class reluctantly, and only because his wife had coaxed him to try it "just this once." Jack had also been contacted by Bob a few times, and he was embarrassed to make up any more excuses.

The house they approached was a typical suburban home, much like their own. This was some relief, for Jack was uncomfortable in too elegant a home. When they rang the bell the door opened almost too quickly. It was obvious they were expected, and others were there ahead of them. Bob introduced himself and made Jack feel very welcome. A few quick introductions moved them into the living room. Some already had a cup of coffee in their hand as they stood or sat chatting.

As class time began it wasn't Bob who took charge, but Mike. He urged them to find seats and be comfortable. Mike suggested for the sake of the guests, "Let us share our names, occupation and something about our family." Jack found the atmosphere very casual and relaxing.

This was the beginning of what proved to be a life-changing experience for Jack. He found it altogether too interesting that first night to resist coming again. The process of interpersonal communication that took place as the Bible came alive in terms of application, led him to accept Christ as his personal Saviour a few weeks later.

External Barriers — Atmosphere

Mike, the class leader, and Bob and Jane would be quick to tell you that it was not always this effective. They had learned the hard way that there are many barriers to good communication. They had first met in the large basement room with chairs set up in rows. Mike had tried to lecture and then get some interaction. The atmosphere was stiff and formal. Those who were invited soon made excuses not to return.

After sharing with other leaders at the monthly church meeting, Mike and his partners learned to make some important changes. They moved from the basement to the living room and their group grew. When their number exceeded twelve, they divided into two groups within the same home so all could participate.

External Barriers — People with Differences

June had been attending class for many weeks with very little involvement in the discussion. She wasn't normally so reticent to speak up. Mary asked her one day why she didn't share more. June hesitated a moment, then said, "I suppose it's because Dr. Mason is in our group. I just can't get personal with him there."

This kind of image barrier to communication shows up in many forms. Some people have strong feelings towards others

82

in different religious backgrounds. A defensive or judgmental spirit creeps into the conversation. It is difficult to look past the religious label to discover the real person behind it. This also may happen when peoples of different race or culture are present. These communication barriers need to be faced and become part of the open, honest sharing in the group.

One of the most common external barriers to communication is the religious language used by many Christians. Raised from childhood in the atmosphere of the church where Christian terminology is as natural as breathing, these Christians sometimes have difficulty appreciating that many people find their terminology foreign and strange. They may reason that surely it is all right to use biblical language when reading the Bible together, but newcomers need introduction to these words and their meaning in the process of study and discussion.

Internal Barriers — Emotional Problems

Bruce had an automatic reflex in almost every human encounter. He could not remember, from earliest childhood, ever doing anything right. The negative, nagging atmosphere of childhood seemed to be reinforced by everybody he met. It didn't occur to Bruce that it was his own poor self-image that created so much hassle. In Bible class he tended to dominate the conversation. It was hard for him to listen to others; and when they did speak, he felt threatened by what they said. With a great deal of patience the group enabled Bruce to reach a point where he could trust them and share his deep frustration. In this atmosphere of open honesty he discovered he could exchange his self-image for a new image in Christ. When he invited Christ into his life, he had a new point of reference, "Not I, but Christ."

Not everyone's poor self-image is so obvious. Nor do people express it the same way. Many people hide behind masks to cover up their insecurity. These masks hide many different symptoms:

83

The fear of being ignored — "If I say something they won't hear me out."

Fear of exposure — "I'm a poor reader. I can't pray out loud. I don't know much about the Bible."

Hurt emotions — "If I share my feelings you might not respond or you might belittle me."

The high cost of involvement — "I have troubles enough of my own, why should I listen to yours?"

Agenda anxiety — "We have to cover the material."

None of us is exempt from emotional problems. Unless we have opportunity to bring our personal "hang-ups" out into the open, we will have less chance of overcoming them and enjoying the kind of life which God intends for us. Each of us needs other people with whom we can interact to get a realistic view of ourselves and work at overcoming these idiosyncrasies.

We may not always be ready to listen to, or believe, those in our families. And sometimes, if our friends notice an area in our lives that needs improvement, they may steer clear of mentioning it, for fear that doing so might threaten the friendship.

But where the Bible is the standard, and everyone is working together to build their lives according to objective biblical standards, then the Holy Spirit can produce the necessary conviction, and these personal problems can be dealt with. The give and take in dialogue furnishes the means to apply solutions that are based on the Word of God.

Here is how this process worked in the lives of one of our men. He said, "I have been a Christian since my youth and felt I was quite mature in my faith. Not until I got into dialogue in a Bible class did I discover deep-seated resentments that were affecting all my life patterns."

Another person confessed, "My mother was always after me to get things done. I didn't realize before that I turn my wife off when she asks me to do something. I see it isn't fair to make her a victim of my childhood hang-ups."

Bearing Each Other's Burdens

Paul said, "Bear ye one another's burdens and thus fulfill the law of Christ" (Gal. 6:2). We need to consider this injunction as it relates to dialogue. Burdens too often are considered external or material. The greatest burdens, however, are internal and emotional. To share these burdens may be very costly for both parties involved.

Because our personalities are so inseparably linked to the way we feel, any attempt to change emotions is a threat to our existence. It is precisely because dialogue reaches to the very heart of human personality and effects meaningful change and creativity, that some people feel threatened and back away.

People can share their inner personalities with others only when they feel that they can trust the others in their small group. As biblical truth is applied to life situations, and people see the inconsistencies between their lives and the biblical standards, there may at first be defensive reactions. These are sometimes expressed through feelings of shame, or hurt, or even anger. Healing takes place as the group holds together in patient love while these inner emotions are brought out into the open.

When the inner self can be exposed and shared with Christ, then people can experience the exchanged life with Him. That is the meaning of Christ's challenge to His disciples, "For whosoever will save his life shall lose it: but whosoever will lose his life for my sake, the same shall save it" (Luke 9:24). As people are willing to "lose" their lives by being open to other believers and to God through the power of the Holy Spirit, Christ stands ready to offer them a whole new set of emotions which are beautifully described in Galatians 5 as the "fruit of the spirit" — love, joy, peace, longsuffering, gentleness, goodness, faith, meekness and temperance (see Gal. 5:22, 23).

Results of Dialogue — Changed Lives

The most exciting and rewarding experience, resulting from small group dialogues, is seeing converts come to Christ. Let me share the experience of Helen as she saw it take place in one of her classes.

"When I was first approached about taking a class I wanted to run and hide, and I think I did for a while. Well, my impulse was to leave that kind of stuff to those who were really talented in speaking or someone who was a dynamic leader. I was sure that I was neither of those, so I felt I was safe. But as I took this before the Lord, He convinced me that it was not my talents or even my lack of talents He wanted — He just wanted a channel. And so it was with this thought in mind that I began my first class. My textbook was the Gospel of Mark. No commentaries and notes from the pastor. Just little ole me, and the Lord. Perhaps it was because I wasn't filled to the brim with knowledge and I wasn't overflowing with keen ideas that the Lord really blessed our class. I actually had little to say, but yet the miracle of dialogue was taking place. It was exciting and stimulating, the Lord was just blessing day after day.

"We opened the Bible, and we asked two simple questions: 'What does it say?' and, 'What does it say to me?' Later my first class suggested that we add another question: 'What does it say to me for today, for this specific day?' Then towards the end of the year they wanted to add another one: 'How did it change my life last week?' It was changing their lives. It was changing my life too. We learned to listen to each other — not just to words, but to the lives behind the words. In listening to others I found that my own need was being voiced and met also.

"We allowed everyone to state their own opinions, and they were able to do this without defense. I think it is very necessary to create this freedom within the group. The natural response to listening to each other is to open God's Word and listen to it. To me this is true dialogue, sharing lives with each other around the Word, then relating the truth from God's Word and appropriating it for our needs. We allowed the Bible to speak for itself. You can't go wrong with this rule. I didn't

86

need to interpret it for the group. I felt the Holy Spirit was fully adequate to do this. By the end of the first year I was encouraged and almost startled as I sat back to see the changes within the group.

"The second year will always shine in my memory; it was there that two of the girls found Christ as their Saviour. Now I had known the Lord for fifteen years, and actually I had never gotten out of my shell and gone and told anyone about the Lord. I was just so selfish; I kept it all to myself. We were studying in the Gospel of John — they had encountered Christ in Mark the year before and now as they read the third chapter about Nicodemus they saw that they had a need, they needed salvation. They related the Scripture to their own life, and there they found Him. I witnessed this miracle, and I have never forgotten the freshness of that moment."

Part Three

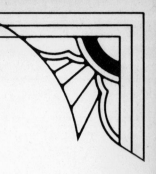

HOW TO START HOME BIBLE STUDIES
THROUGH YOUR CHURCH

How do I start home Bible study groups
through my church? Where does the home Bible class
concept fit in with the rest of the church program?

If you have been asking these questions,
you'll find the answers here.
The home Bible class is the means
through which dialogue
can take place in the church.

Chapters 8, 9 and 10 describe in detail
where dialogue fits in with the rest
of the church program, how to organize home
Bible classes and how to run them. Read this and
you will be better equipped
to begin implementing changes that could bring
new life to your church.

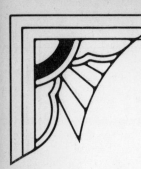

8

PREACHING, TEACHING AND DIALOGUE — IT TAKES ALL THREE

There are at least three basic means of communicating the gospel in the total life of the church. The church-shaped diagram (Sketch A) relates them to each other in order.

Preaching to Inspire and Edify

A great deal may be said about the content and manner of preaching, but one thing remains true: The command to preach the gospel comes to us both from Jesus Himself, and in the writings of all the apostles. Preaching has held, and will always hold, a central position in the body of the church. "It pleased God, by the foolishness of preaching to save them that believe" (1 Cor. 1:21).

Much has been written concerning preaching in its various forms and practices. Men have attained great prominence both in the church and in society through the practice of preaching.

CHURCH LIFE

PREACHING
- Inspiration
- Edification

TEACHING
- Learning
- Training

DIALOGUE
- Fellowship
- Evangelism

SKETCH A

Traditionally, preaching has been accompanied by good music. Music in like manner has played a prominent part in the history of the church. Music sets the stage. It prepares the heart. It enables the person to be responsive and ready for the preaching that follows.

Most evangelists have a soloist or musician who accompanies them. Most churches have their choirs, soloists and musical accompanists. Martin Luther gave music a high compliment when he said, "More people are won into the Kingdom of God through music than through my preaching."

It was the apostle Paul who said, "In the mouth of two or three witnesses shall every word be established" (2 Cor. 13:1). Special meetings in the local church enable God to establish truth through guest speakers in addition to the local pastor. Special speakers may not add any new truths to what the pastor has already spoken, but in the second proclamation of the same truth hearts can be moved by the Holy Spirit in a fresh way. Congregations need the testimony of added voices to complement and supplement the regular preaching ministry.

Teaching should not be the most important objective of a sermon. A close look at the church and Holy Scriptures indicates that preaching has two elements in it that are more significant than teaching. These are: *inspiration* and *edification.*

Christians go to church to have a meeting with God. They expect to hear God's Word preached (see Sketch B). But it is not enough that the doctrines and theology and teachings of Scripture should be proclaimed. People are also looking for the Word of God to be clothed with humanity. They want to be *inspired* to live the Christian life.

Daniel Webster was reprimanded by his pastor in Washington, D.C. because he had not been in church for a while. Daniel Webster replied, "I go out into the country on Sunday to the little church there. When I come to the church in the city you speak to Daniel Webster the Senator. When I go to the lit-

PREACHING

INSPIRATION
EDIFICATION

Pulpit Ministry

tle country church the pastor speaks to Daniel Webster the sinner."

Christians also need to be *edified*. The word "edify" is used to describe the process of promoting spiritual growth and character development of believers by teaching or example. In the struggle of life Christians need to be helped and lifted up and strengthened to go in their Christian life and walk. If there is anything the preacher needs, it is the anointing of the Holy Spirit that enables him to speak as an oracle of God to the hearts of men. No matter how scholarly a sermon may be, if it lacks the Spirit's anointing, it fails to edify the human heart.

I would not imply by this that sermons should not be scholarly. I believe with all my heart that the first responsibility of the preacher is to spend a great deal of time in study and research and glean everything that he can from a text before he proclaims it. It has been my practice in the many years of my ministry to study twenty hours a week in preparation for my Sunday morning sermon. I have been pastoring in the same church for twenty-four years and am still practicing that principle. There is no room for laziness or lack of scholarship in preaching.

Teaching Through the Home

The teaching ministry of the church should be threefold: the home, the Sunday School and specialized training. In the sixth chapter of Deuteronomy Moses laid down the principles and practices of training in the home (see Deut. 6:6,7). Enough cannot be said of the importance of parents training their children from earliest infancy in the warm atmosphere of the Christian home. It was in reference to the home that Holy Scripture makes the promise, "Train up a child in the way he should go: and when he is old he will not depart from it" (Prov. 22:6).

Teaching Through the Sunday School

In recent generations the emphasis on Christian education

in the church has been directed through the Sunday School. My experience has been that the Sunday School can be the most effective training agency in the life of the church. The proper quality of teachers and curriculum in the Sunday School has a profound effect upon the lives of both children and adults. The adult department should use a Bible curriculum to prepare students to become leaders and teachers in the church.

Note carefully that when we speak of the teaching ministry of the church, we are referring to teachers who are resource persons for the subject matter, guiding a group of pupils in the learning process. Although a versatile teacher can use a great many methods and tools for effective teaching, nevertheless, in the Sunday School setting, he remains the principal resource person and authority figure. The solid lines in Sketch C illustrate the teacher as a key resource and facilitator in the class. The dotted lines illustrate possible opportunities for group interaction resulting from the input of the teacher.

Teaching Through Leadership Training

Supplementing the home and the Sunday School is the area of Christian education I am referring to as special training. Some churches have a "training hour," which is usually on a Sunday night preceding or following the evening service. A multiplicity of curriculum may be used, but the primary purpose of the training hour is to develop leaders in various areas of the church life. (We should also take advantage of every form of help that comes to us in local conventions, in denominational programming and in the seminars that are developed across the nation. Campus Crusade, Basic Youth Conflicts, International Center for Learning and other agencies are a great help to the local church.)

Fellowship/Evangelism Through Dialogue

The third area of ministering the gospel in the church is dialogue. The purpose of dialogue is to lead people into open,

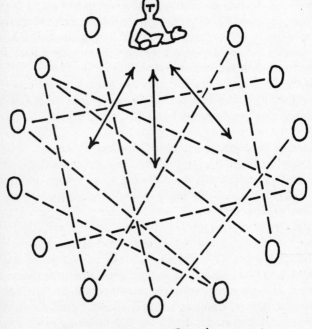

TEACHING
LEARNING
TRAINING

Sunday School
Training Hour

SKETCH C

honest sharing so as to produce deep levels of Christian fellowship and personal involvement. Dialogue produces applied faith in an atmosphere of Christian community. This atmosphere of open and honest sharing with one another is what constitutes the essence of the home Bible class procedure.

There are two things that a leader of a home Bible class is not. He or she is not a resource person who prepares materials through extensive study and research, and comes to share that material with the class. This would make the leader a lecturer and would destroy the principle of dialogue in the group. Secondly, the leader is not the authority in the group. An authority figure will always cause the group to turn to him for final decision.

Rather, in dialogue the leader places himself on an equal with the other members of the class (see Sketch D). Each member of the class looks to the one source and to the one authority, the Bible. Dialogue is always Bible centered. The leader sees that the group is always relating the Bible to their personal lives.

We are hearing a great deal these days on the return of the spiritual gifts to the body of Christ. It is in the home Bible class atmosphere that the church can best share these spiritual gifts and minister one to another. This results in the development of Christian character and affords a seedbed for evangelism.

Changing Lives

When Christians are genuinely sharing their faith as it is practiced in every experience of daily life, then unchurched friends can be invited into this atmosphere and discover that Christianity is very much alive. Christ is working in the lives of these that are meeting together. The old song, "What the world needs is Jesus, just a glimpse of Him," comes through loud and clear when Christians, via dialogue, are sharing the implications of the Christian life for the nitty-gritty of everyday.

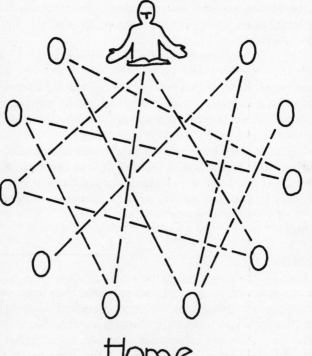

DIALOGUE
FELLOWSHIP
EVANGELISM

Home
Bible Classes

This was clearly illustrated when a man involved in a home Bible class was so excited in his new experiences in Christian faith he shared them with a dentist friend. The friend became sufficiently curious to accept an invitation to attend the Bible class the following Monday. In the casual, homey atmosphere he was introduced to the various people in the class. He found that most of the members were of the same level of education as himself, mostly professionals. Leading the class was a local judge. As he observed what was going on in the class that evening, he was puzzled at the way they used the Bible.

When class was over and his friend was driving him home the dentist asked the question, "How can intelligent people like you regard the Bible as being the authority? Why do you talk about this man, Jesus, as though He was alive?" The friend made no attempt to prove the truth of the Bible or the reality of the living Christ. He just urged him to continue to come to the class and see for himself.

In the next class, the dentist challenged the group in their use of the Bible as authority and questioned their talking of Christ as being alive. Again he discovered that they did not come to the defense of the Bible, nor did they argue about the resurrected and living Christ. They simply encouraged him to share with them what they were reading in the Bible. Deeply puzzled, he thought they were playing some kind of a game.

By the end of class his curiosity had become a concern. He said to his friend, "You don't need to pick me up next week, I'll be here on my own." Halfway through the next class the dentist was so moved emotionally and so disturbed that he said to the class, "I don't understand what is going on here, but you people have something that I have never seen or experienced before. What is it?"

They simply replied, "We have the Lord Jesus."

He said, "How can I have the Lord Jesus?" And there in the class they were able to lead him to a personal acceptance of Jesus Christ as his Saviour and Lord.

The class did not defend the Bible nor explain doctrines. Yet the reality of Christ in their lives came through loud and clear from the Word which convicted the man of his need of a Saviour. The Christian faith in dialogue gives a natural atmosphere in which the unsaved can discover the person of Jesus Christ.

One Structure — Three Parts

Looking back now at the diagram, we have the three parts of the total church life in perspective: First, the preaching ministry is to inspire and edify the body of Christ with an element of teaching. Second, the teaching ministry is to guide and instruct students in discovering and applying the Word to their everyday experiences, and to train leadership. The third part of church life is dialogue. This is carried on in small groups in homes where individuals can be involved one with another at the deep level of their personal lives, sharing the application of the Word of God in every part of daily living.

Here with applied faith and adherence to the Word, Christians grow and minister to one another, and the resultant atmosphere is ideal for bringing in unchurched neighbors and friends so they too can discover the reality of Christ in their lives.

9
HOW TO ORGANIZE
HOME BIBLE CLASSES

From its very beginning, the New Testament church in the house was conducted under the supervision of the apostles and was subject to their preaching and teaching. The apostle Paul was careful to instruct Titus and Timothy to ordain elders who would oversee the churches meeting in homes. Right from the start, these groups were guided and supervised by shepherds.

The Commitment of the Pastor

Today the key person in any home Bible class ministry must be the local pastor. As shepherd of his flock, he must have a vision of what could happen in his church and in the lives of his people through this kind of involvement. He must see the value to his ministry, he must have a vision of the potential, and he must be willing to count the cost in terms of the investment of personal time and energy in the lives of those who will be called upon to be group leaders.

The benefits are many. Every leader in a home Bible class will become, in a very real sense, an extension of the pastor, ministering to small groups and building on the pastor's teaching. Through the ministry of the groups, as people are brought into the fold, there will be opportunity to shepherd and encourage those evangelized through the care and attention given by the group leaders.

The pastor's role will also provide a source of stability on the conduct of the groups. It is true that small groups meeting in the privacy of homes, apart from the pastor's direct guidance, can be a source of problems. Novices, unskilled leadership, heretical views could create problems. By meeting regularly with the leaders and being aware of what's happening in the groups, the pastor can help to ensure that these kinds of problems do not develop.

Selecting the Leadership

The initial and ongoing role of the pastor in the home Bible class ministry will be his relationship with the group leaders. The first step, therefore, in organizing home Bible classes in the church must be the careful selection of leaders. The pastor should not call for volunteers, but should select those in the church family he deems most effective in giving leadership to this kind of program. To ask for volunteers, allowing anyone to share in leadership, could be detrimental to the program and produce embarrassing results. The pastor should go over his church membership carefully and prayerfully, looking to the Lord for wisdom as to whom to select.

What makes a person qualified to lead a home Bible study? Not necessarily "leadership ability," if by leadership ability we mean someone who can take charge in a group and dominate it. Rather, the leader of a home Bible study should be someone with heart, someone who cares for people, and who is secure enough in his own relationship with God that he doesn't "need" the leadership position in order to prop up his own identity. Sometimes the best leaders are those who are willing, but don't really think they can do it. This is the kind of person God can work through.

The leadership should come from all ages ranging from high school and above. High school and college age young people are quite effective in conducting these small dialogue groups. Women should be selected to conduct the classes for women's groups meeting during the day, while men should be selected for the couples groups and mixed age groups meeting during the evenings.

Training the Leadership

Having carefully selected the people suited for training, the pastor should invite them to share in a weekly training session. The purpose of these sessions is to inform the potential leaders of the basic philosophy behind the home Bible classes. These meetings are an opportunity for the pastor's interest and enthusiasm to be spread to the leaders of the classes. The degree to which they catch his interest and vision is the degree to which the program will be effective, because, in the long run, it all depends on them.

When people are already busy, you can do a lot to ease their schedules by trying to have these sessions in conjunction with some other function at the church, so as not to take up another complete evening. One possibility is to have them concurrent with the regular Wednesday night midweek prayer service. Perhaps, when people in the prayer meeting are divided up into smaller prayer groups, the leaders could go to a separate room for a training session. This way, they wouldn't be detained more than a half hour beyond the time they usually spend at church on a prayer meeting night. If the midweek service cannot be adjusted to accommodate this training period, the Sunday School hour can be used or an hour prior to, or following, the evening service.

The author's book, *How to Conduct Home Bible Classes,*[1] is a helpful tool which you can use as a basic guideline for training. By giving your people specific reading assignments from the book each week, the pastor will be encouraging them to become more involved in the concept. Then, during the sessions, he can allow for interchange and discussion of what they have read. The pastor will, of course, have to do some lecturing during this training time. However, by drawing people into discussion and dialogue, he can effectively model ways the classes can be conducted.

The number of weeks necessary for this training procedure will largely be dependent on the nature of the group, the quality of input, and the degree of commitment they give it. Hopefully, six to eight weeks should be adequate.

Setting Up the Classes

Not all of those who take this training will want to become leaders in home Bible classes right away. In one sense this is an advantage, because those not ready to lead may be willing to be the host and invite groups to meet in their homes. The leader and host thus give team cooperation in the home Bible class, both being trained. As the classes grow in the homes, and division becomes necessary, the logical person to take over the additional groups would be the hosts, who, having been trained, and now comfortable with the program, feel at ease to take a more active part.

When the leaders are ready to begin classes, their natural tendency seems to be the desire to invite the unchurched, so they can share the excitement of evangelism. An immediate result will be new converts. However, the pastor must be very careful at this point and not allow the fledgling program to begin with the majority of outsiders making up the classes. This is an important precaution. The congregation may not be ready to receive previously unchurched and newly-converted people coming through the dialogical setting when their own frame of reference is totally monological.

It is wise and I strongly urge, therefore, that the first preparation in organizing classes be geared to meeting the need of the local congregation. The home Bible class program will prepare the local congregation to share a quality of interpersonal relationship and depth of spiritual concern for one another that will enable them as a body to absorb new converts.

Promotion for the home Bible classes should begin from the pulpit, the pastor outlining the merits of the program and encouraging the people to identify themselves with it, and respond to the invitations they receive to join the classes. The names of church members should be divided among the leaders and hosts for their personal invitation.

Initially, a large percentage of the congregation may not respond. This is not the kind of program that mushrooms into existence overnight and flourishes. Getting the program going demands patient work with some pilot programming to demonstrate its worth. This enables those who hear about it to recognize what the Lord is doing in the groups. A degree of patience is needed both by the pastor and the leaders as the program gets underway. The quality of spiritual life gendered in the class is its own best promotion for growth and continuance.

Generally, there is no need to distinguish between age, education, or profession as to who attends what class, although high schoolers usually are best organized separately. In time, certain kinds of people may gravitate toward specific classes, but this does not need to be a disturbing factor as there is a built-in method to rearrange the class participants as the program develops.

Building Unity and Trust

Keep a group together for three to six months to develop a strong level of trust and sharing before making any attempt to bring in people outside the church. The effectiveness of the group to influence unchurched people and non-Christians to receive Christ is directly proportionate to the level of trust and love that is shared in the group. To bring the outsider in while those in the class are still in the process of trying to develop

105

this strong personal relationship can be devastating in its effect on the newcomer. It will require considerable time for Christians to depart from their objective impersonal discussion of biblical truth and progress to a level of deep applied scriptural practice.

This quality of sharing must be present if evangelism is to be effective. Head knowledge alone does not make a Christian. Not until the whole personality is committed to Jesus Christ does the Holy Spirit have the freedom to do His work in convicting of sin, righteousness, and judgment, and moving the individual into the Christian life.

Initiating Evangelism

After a level of penetration has been reached in the local congregation producing the effect of freedom and sharing in the larger body, then it is time to strongly promote the evangelistic thrust throughout the home Bible classes. Not all leaders and groups will be effective in this area. Some Christians could remain so locked into theological language and so negative in their relationship to others that they will be ineffective in making the unchurched comfortable in their midst. If the unchurched do not sense they are being appreciated as persons, even though many of those in the group may not agree with their life-style and values, they will not sense the presence of the Holy Spirit and will not be drawn to Jesus Christ.

As Christians we bask in the reality of God's unconditional love towards us in that He loves us as persons even when He hates some of our conduct. Nevertheless, we find it difficult to pass on this same quality of love to those around us. Hopefully, in time, this becomes the by-product of the interaction in dialogue in the group.

Mixing the Groups

Three types of classes will probably evolve. The young people either meeting at the church or in the privacy of homes; the women meeting through the day and possibly a working woman's group in the evening; and the various groups for all ages in the evening.

When the program has been going successfully for a year, it becomes necessary to institute a method to ensure that the groups do not become ingrown and cliquish. The classes should be encouraged to abandon activities during the months of July and August. This will allow an opportunity to regroup when they reorganize in September or October. A wise policy would be that not more than fifty percent of those who were in the group as they disbanded be allowed to join with the same group as it reorganizes. The additional number needed to make a class from each half of the split group should come from others being invited in from the church body and from outside the church. This stimulates new life and exchange in the class. It enlivens the dialogue and extends the spiritual fellowship. This process can be nicely promoted by calling it "fruit basket upset."

Meeting Regularly with the Leadership

To maintain strong healthy classes the pastor should make it his fixed policy to meet with the leaders and hosts on a regular basis. In the original organizing of the program the pastor may find it advisable to continue the weekly meeting until confidence is sufficiently established in the leaders and hosts. Once that level has been reached, the pastor should continue to meet on a regular (usually monthly) basis with the leaders. Again, caution should be taken not to demand extra nights out by the leaders, but rather to adapt this meeting to the existent program as mentioned before.

Limit the meeting to an hour in length. A portion of the time should be input by the pastor, as he sees needs and seeks to promote certain things within the program. At least half the time should be given to the leaders and hosts to share with each other, both by way of problem solving and in encouraging one another. Exciting experiences continually occur in the groups and find expression in the monthly meetings.

The pastor's continuous relationship to the groups is maintained through these monthly meetings. Failure to keep in close contact with leaders may lead to groups drifting from their commitment to the church and pastor. These monthly meetings are the primary method of control and direction of the groups. The monthly meeting also allows the pastor to evaluate the spiritual health of each group. With the counsel of the leader, he will be able to determine when a group is in a position to launch out into evangelism. Some groups may arrive at that level within three months. Most however will require at least six months. Some may never quite get to that level.

When the pastor feels the group is ready, he should then urge them to invite unchurched into the class. Those whose children are in Sunday School, or whose young people are involved in the youth program, are a good starting place. They already have some connection with the church. These people will usually respond to an invitation.

The second area of contacts could be the homes immediately surrounding those areas where the groups are meeting. Some hosts invite their neighbors to their home for a social evening and then tell them about the group which meets there weekly. An invitation is extended for the neighbors to come and see what the group is doing. Some leaders have made written invitations and distributed them to their neighbors. Ladies' daytime groups have had social teas for the neighbors, informing them of the group meeting, and inviting them to return. Many methods may be used.

Whenever there is a community-wide evangelistic outreach, people in need of follow-up should certainly be invited into the small groups. Nothing is quite so effective in helping the converts of an evangelistic campaign as the personalized love and concern shared in the small groups in a home.

Selecting a Coordinator

If the program takes root and starts to grow, there will come a time, after approximately a year, when the large number of groups will need more detailed care than the pastor, with his many other responsibilities, can give. At this time he should be watching for a person who has leadership ability, genuine concern for the entire program, and holds the respect and confidence of the congregation. Such a person should be singled out and trained to become a coordinator. His primary function would be to work with the pastor to oversee the operation of the program.

It is the coordinator who assists in setting up the classes as they begin in the fall. He has a list of all the previous leaders, hosts and participants. He helps to rearrange the groupings. He personally solicits the assistance of those who have been in the program and appear to have potential for leadership.

The coordinator also sees that monthly reports listing the groups' participants are turned in by the leaders and hosts. He keeps a filing system noting where groups are meeting. He works towards a further saturation of the church family, involving more people in the classes. It is further his responsibility to keep records of the procedure of the classes.

The coordinator keeps continually abreast of the growth and divisions of the classes. He watches over the new and developing leaders in order to maintain a constant reserve of potential leaders for the expanding groups. He has access to the names and locations of all those who are potential leaders and sees that the classes are provided with adequate leadership. Any action that he may take in this regard, he shares with the pastor and together they decide who should be leading.

The coordinator should be a by-product of the classes themselves. If he is going to be effective in the position he holds, it will be because he has come through the program itself and has demonstrated unusual leadership and ability in the process. Even while serving as coordinator, he should remain in a class and often lead it, just to be involved and to provide a model for the others to follow.

The coordinator not only releases the pastor from much of

the detail, but also maintains the free flow and stable operation of the entire program. With the pastor, he can also gender a great deal of enthusiasm for the continuance of the program.

As the program grows, secretarial help will also be needed to assist the coordinator and pastor in keeping accurate records of all the activities from year to year.

Locating for Growth

Home Bible classes should be geographically located to give the best coverage to the community. At first, of course, when the classes are beginning, there will not be sufficient numbers of them for this to be important. But as the classes expand and multiply, coverage of the community should be the goal.

These classes provide an excellent way to share the gospel in apartment buildings. Because of the semi-isolation of apartment dwellers, home Bible classes have been found to be very effective in getting into apartments, where other methods of evangelism have failed. Classes confined to the apartment complex apparently pose no security threat.

Ideally, the evening classes should be an hour in length. They should start promptly and end on time, in recognition of the fact that everyone's schedule is already crowded. This is especially true when participants have babysitters with their children during the class.

Excelling for God

In setting up these home Bible classes, it is good to keep in mind Paul's injunction to the Corinthians: "Let all things be done properly and in an orderly manner" (1 Cor. 14:40, *NASB*). The work of the ministry of Jesus Christ deserves our very best. The standard of performance must be excellence, not out of a motivation to impress people or to build a reputation, but simply because God deserves the best.

As you pray concerning this ministry and the possibility of getting it started in your church, take time before God to let Him direct you to the right people for leadership, for participation, for serving as hosts or coordinators or any other capacity. There may be discouragements, and sometimes the task may seem too big to handle. Let that serve as a reminder that the ministry is God's, and that it is only by His Spirit that any of this can happen. Remember who it is that is building the church!

Footnote

1. Albert J. Wollen, *How To Conduct Home Bible Classes* (Wheaton, Ill.: Scripture Press Publications, Inc., 1969).

10
HOW TO CONDUCT HOME BIBLE CLASSES

One of the main purposes of having Bible classes in homes is to promote a casual relaxed setting in which people can have the freedom to be themselves. But having a casual, relaxed atmosphere does not rule out having a purpose and a plan on how to achieve it. In fact, to plan for a casual atmosphere probably takes much more careful thought and insight into people's needs than planning for more formal functions. Therefore, it is essential that anyone planning to participate in leading a home Bible class take time to consider the goals and ways to implement them. When we realize the implications of what we are aiming to accomplish in these studies, providing an opportunity for people's lives to be enriched and challenged through exposure to God's Word and to one another, we realize the stakes are high. And every bit of effort in planning will be worth it.

How the Leader Prepares

It is natural to ask what material should be studied in these home Bible classes. Experience has demonstrated that the most effective method of maintaining dialogue in a group is to stay by the simple process, simply looking at Scripture and then discussing it in terms of its personal application: "What does it say?" and "What does it say to me?"

This being the case, certain books of the Bible are more appropriate for the method than others. It is recommended that you begin with the Gospel of Mark, then the Gospel of John, then the First Epistle of John. Following that, any of the shorter books in the New Testament may be used. The book of Hebrews and the book of Revelation should never be used for a home Bible class dialogue, simply because they are so long and because their content does not lend itself to dialogue as well as that of some of the other books. Selected narratives or psalms from the Old Testament could be used, however.

The leader needs to put in some preparation time before the start of the session. He needs to read the passage for a session, usually one chapter, and thoroughly familiarize himself with its content. As he reads, he keeps in mind how he himself would answer the two dialogue questions, "What does the Bible say?" and "What does it say to me?" If the leader has studied the passage in light of these questions and found areas in his own life where the passage speaks to him, this will help him have a better idea on how to draw people into the passage during the session.

After going through the passage in this way, the leader will need to decide what paragraph divisions to use. Sometimes the paragraphs are marked differently in different versions, and in others, they are not marked at all. For each paragraph the leader should choose a small selection of verses which focus on a single incident or theme in the text.

As the leader is preparing, he should jot down several questions that could be used to stimulate discussion. These should not be "thought" questions, but strictly "knowledge" questions — questions which help people identify specific things happening in the text. These would all fall under the category of the general question: "What does the Bible say?"

Leaders should remember not to use their position as a launching pad for the dissemination of their own particular theological views or personal Christian "hobby horses." The home Bible class concept depends strongly on allowing people the freedom, under the guidance of the Holy Spirit, to approach the Bible in as honest and objective a way as possible. It is this kind of honest searching in the Scriptures that is most likely to grow into opportunities for dialogue.

By having thought through a series of questions, leaders will be able to anticipate where the class will go. The object should not be to "get through all the questions," but to use them as springboards for stimulating response from the people in the group. Leaders should be careful to resist the impulse to answer their own questions, especially if no one responds immediately. Rather than answering the question, the leader might restate it in a different way so as to encourage participation from the group.

Concerning preparation for the second question, "What does it say to me?" the leader needs to have considered this personally in his own study. His initiative in sharing some of his own needs as the Scripture speaks to him will encourage others to participate also.

How the Class Is Conducted

The setting in the local home should be casual, an atmosphere in which those who come can feel comfortable. The living room seems the natural choice for a place to meet. However, sometimes groups prefer the dining room where they can have their Bibles before them on a table, and where the relationship is a little closer.

As the guests arrive it will be the responsibility of the host to greet them at the door and make them feel welcome and comfortable. If a new person is joining the group, time should be taken for introductions and some casual personal sharing in order to make the newcomer feel at ease. The host should provide extra copies of the Bible for guests who may arrive without one. Everyone should have a Bible as the group begins. A variety of versions is helpful so that in the process of discussion there can be reference to the various ways in which the passage is stating its truth. This also gives a greater opportunity for the group to interact with one another as they read the various versions.

The first question that normally arises regarding class procedure is: Should the class open with prayer? To begin with, when there are newcomers and the spiritual level of the group is not known, it is much wiser to allow prayer to come out of the discussion of the text they are reading, rather than imposing a form upon the group from the beginning. If the group develops its own sense of the worth of prayer and desires to begin with prayer, then that is completely in order. The groups that are highly evangelistic and are bringing outsiders in should not automatically bring prayer into their activity until the newcomers are adequately introduced to it.

Two simple ground rules need to be explained as the groups get under way. First, *the Bible is to be shared in dialogue.* There is no teacher in the class. No one is acting as an authority to which the rest of the group must turn for answers. Everyone, including the leader, is meeting on an equal basis.

Second, *the only authority in the group is the Bible.* It must be recognized as the point of reference for all things and always regarded as the final decision in any matter of discussion. Everyone's opinion will be equally respected. The class is not a place to argue or to prove someone is right and someone is wrong. It is a place in which to simply look at the biblical content and then discuss the implications in terms of our personal lives. Two key questions that will dominate the entire time: *"What does the Bible say?"* and secondly, *"What does it say to me?"*

The Gospel of Mark should be used in all classes as their

115

starting point. There are several reasons why the Gospel of Mark is most useful. It has no opening genealogy, nor does it have the weighty prologue. It introduces the person of Jesus Christ, around which the entire discussion and application should center.

"What Does the Bible Say?"

To begin the class the leader calls for a volunteer or names someone in the group to read the section of verses. Never should the leader name someone to read until it is obvious the person is perfectly free and willing to be called upon in that manner. The leader must be very sensitive and never offend or lead in such a way that might cause a person to clam up, withdraw from the activity or stop sharing in the class.

The paragraph or section of verses may be read in any version depending on the volunteer. After the reading of the paragraph, the leader launches a question regarding what the text says. As the group responds, the leader makes sure the group stays with the biblical text. After the leader has launched the question he should guide the group's discussion of that question. Then when he feels there has been sufficient discussion, he should smoothly summarize the response and lead into the next question.

It usually requires a series of questions to adequately bring to light the content of the passage. But at no time should the leader feel responsible to answer the question he has launched. Nor should he allow himself to answer side questions that someone may raise, for in so doing he may inadvertently divest the Scripture of its authority and assume the authority role himself. The Scripture should always answer for itself.

Although someone may feel a particular truth should be stressed, no unusual emphasis should be placed on that truth. Rather, leaders should let self-evident truths rise naturally from the discussion. There may also be a tendency for some Christians to try to establish their particular views on certain scriptural points and disprove the views of others. A wise leader will draw the discussion graciously back to the text itself and again ask, "What does the text say?" This will avoid the extravagances of individual interpretation upon the text.

"What Does It Say to Me?"

After a sufficient time is spent discussing the content of the text the leader puts forth the question, "What does it say to me?" The personal application is necessary if there is going to be any meaningful dialogue in the group. Discussion does not imply dialogue. One may discuss at length any subject without any personal involvement with the subject of the discussion. Not until the subject matter has been exposed to the human personality and personally applied can real dialogue begin to take place. The leader's role here is to encourage individuals to respond to the content in terms of their personal experiences.

For example, in the first paragraph of the Gospel of Mark certain words have very strong personal implication. The word *baptism,* though practiced in various methods, can be of personal significance to each individual. The focus here could be on people's own experiences and attitudes in relation to baptism. Mark also talks about "repentance," and certainly, if there are Christians present, they could share about their personal experiences of genuine repentance. The conversation should not be allowed to bog down in the theological implications of repentance but should be replete with personal repentance experiences. John the Baptist speaks of forgiveness of sin in that first paragraph. The group could share personal experiences of the sense of forgiveness of sin and the release from guilt.

When a paragraph has been read, discussed and some level of dialogue reached, then the leader should move the group to the next paragraph. It is better to cover more Scripture than bog down in too much detailed examination of one paragraph. A good rule of thumb is that in the hour's time the group should have covered not less than half a chapter and preferably a full chapter.

Prayer will automatically be introduced in the process of reading the Scripture. It will be discussed among the group as to what practice exists in their lives. Out of that discussion comes a natural response to pray for individuals expressing need in the group. Prayer should become spontaneous so that when someone shares a need there will be a natural pause to remember and pray for this person's need. In this natural conversational manner, prayer will find its own level and will intensify as the group grows together.

Before concluding the class, the leader may want to offer suggestions as to what to read in preparation for the next meeting. This would encourage them to read ahead in the biblical text and to formulate some personal ideas regarding what it says. A typical assignment might be: Look over the next chapter and see what answers you get to the questions, "What does the Bible say?" and "What does it say to me?" Emphasize that this is an optional assignment, and that it need not take a lot of time.

It is not wise to assign in-depth study assignments between classes. If some people have prepared and others haven't, the prepared ones could carry the conversation, and the unprepared ones would feel left out. The class would then become subject oriented rather than person oriented. Also, it is hard to invite new people into a setting where the routine involves extensive preparation. The new people, when they do come, feel as if they aren't really involved, because they don't have as much information as the rest of the group.

When the hour is up, the host can best conclude the hour by bringing in refreshments. Some groups have coffee, tea or soft drinks available when the group arrives, but it is best to keep the refreshments for the end of the class and serve them as a conclusion.

A word of warning. When a group tends to serve fancy desserts, competition can produce stress among the groups as some may try to out-do one another. The wise thing is to maintain the policy that only cookies will be served with the drink.

The leaders should be punctual in starting and closing the class on time so that anyone who has responsibilities or appointments feels free to leave. However, it is not uncommon in many of the groups that some will linger after the dismissal. Occasionally the most effective personal sharing and in-depth spiritual experience takes place on one-to-one basis after the class is over.

How to Plan for Growth

As new people are invited into the class and the class multiplies in size, division will be necessary. A class is only functional in dialogue when it does not number more than twelve. A class that grows beyond this number should be broken into two groups, meeting in the same home but in different rooms. Eventually, these classes may each choose to meet in separate homes, using the home of one of the members as a host home.

When dividing the classes in the home, the newest members form one group. This group should in turn start over again at the beginning of the Gospel of Mark while the original group should continue on from where they were in the text. The leader who is most effective and efficient, usually the original leader, should go with the new group. A new leader taken from the original group can continue with the older group who are well qualified to continue Bible in dialogue with very little assist from the leader. It is often at this point that the host takes the responsibility of leading the group. Should no one in the group be qualified or willing to lead, then the coordinator should be contacted to provide leadership. New growth is the secret for the success of the home Bible class program. As classes divide, more areas of the community are reached. In time this makes it possible for the church to have a home Bible class located in every geographical section of the community in which the church functions.

No great effort should be made to urge the people who are

in the home Bible classes to come to church on Sunday. However, it is very natural and spontaneous that as the lives of those who are in the class are deepened, or find Christ as Saviour, they will gravitate to the church represented by the group. This becomes the natural, normal process in the group.

Members of the group need not be reticent to share their church affiliation and certainly should not be ashamed to make reference to their church life and activity. This does not scare people off, providing you do not make it obvious that you are trying to get them to the church through your home. It should not be a sales gimmick. Genuine spiritual sharing of Christ, not sales gimmickry, attracts people to the church.

How It's Happened Before

The potential for what God can do through a home ministry such as this is limitless. A casual look through the gospel accounts will reveal that Jesus spent much of His time in people's homes, and as a result, many significant things happened. Sick people were healed in people's homes. A dead girl was raised to life in the home of a ruler of the synagogue (see Matt. 9:18—25). In the home of Levi, Jesus associated with "publicans and sinners" (Luke 5:29,30). A woman anointed His feet with ointment while He was in the home of one of the Pharisees and He turned it into an opportunity for honest dialogue (see Luke 7:36—50). John records that Jesus Himself invited some men into the place where He was staying (see John 1:37—39). The home of Lazarus, Mary, and Martha in Bethany, the house that contained the "upper room," the place where Jesus first appeared to the disciples after His resurrection — all these are scenes from the Gospels that take place in people's homes.

Jesus Christ has been at work in people's homes for a long time. He wants to continue that work today. He is waiting to enter any home that is open to Him and to reveal Himself there. What better way is there to invite Him than through a home Bible class?

Epilogue
A FUTURE LOOK

On the west side of the city of Portland there is a ridge of hills that separates the city proper from the Tualatin Valley. As you cross that ridge you have a panoramic view of the entire valley. One day in the early years of my ministry, as I drove over the hill, I parked the car and viewed that magnificent valley below me.

New residential districts were springing up everywhere. Growth was rapid. But there were few churches. The percentage of people attending church was low. Spiritual needs were overwhelming. I cried out in my soul to God, "How can these spiritual needs be met?" I was reminded of Ezekiel when he looked over a valley and heard the Lord say to him, "Son of man, can these bones live?" (Ezek. 37:3).

What has come to pass through the ensuing years has been a great encouragement. Many churches now dot the valley, but more encouraging than this are the many home Bible classes that are meeting in these residential areas. Among the combined churches there are approximately 200 home Bible classes already meeting. The number is growing every month and more and more people are being identified with them. Hopefully, the hour will soon be when there will be a class within walking distance of everybody in the valley.

A Vision for Growth

What is happening in the Tualatin Valley can take place in any community. The state of Oregon has the lowest per-capita church attendance of any state in the Union. It is pleasing God to use this area to demonstrate the effectiveness and outreach of the home Bible class ministry. Hopefully, this ministry will spread throughout the nation. The impact the church could make, when properly organized in small group Bible classes, is tremendous.

Our present society is apathetic in the mundane routine of maintaining the plastic age. Many feel that by and large they are nothing but a number on a computer, a Social Security number, or a credit card number. Life has become so impersonal that most people suffer from the deep pangs of loneliness. There is no warmth of personal relationship from the TV tube. People are bored with the emptiness of their lives.

All this can and must be changed through Christian love and action. Every pastor has the opportunity of multiplying himself in his ministry through the training of home Bible class leaders in his church. Every church has the potential of involving at least seventy-five percent of its congregation in small group Bible studies. And every Bible study group meeting in a home has the potential of creating fellowship involvement that could enable participants to invite their neighbors and friends to attend.

In a fellowship of this kind, there is no place for competition between churches. Christians of various denominations could feel at ease with one another, and have the freedom to share their lives with each other. Unchurched neighbors could sense

122

this warmth and be affected by the spirit of Christian unity. Herein lies the potential of Christ's great prayer in John 17:21, when He said, "That they all may be one; as thou, Father, art in me, and I in thee, that they also may be one in us: that the world may believe that thou hast sent me."

Think of it — Bible classes on every block, a group of Christians meeting in every housing tract, farmers meeting together, businessmen meeting together, blue-collar workers, white-collar workers, youth, adults, people from every walk of life exposed to the powerful truth of God's Word. The time could come when the "in" thing is to attend a home Bible class, where it could be the language of the street to casually ask, "And what home Bible class do you attend?"

A Worldwide Movement

Reports are beginning to filter in from abroad of the small group Bible class movement. In the Philippines, Overseas Crusade has been promoting this type of program through the organization LEGS. During the past two years it is estimated that some 10,000 classes have started. It is still in the experimental stages but most encouraging in its effect thus far.

A report from Haiti in a Baptist publication reads as follows: "The report has come that the churches in Haiti have been 'set on fire' through the springing up of home prayer cells all over the area. Two hundred and eleven Caribbean churches are averaging 500 new converts per month. It all started with prayer cells, each of which divided into two new cells as soon as the number reached twelve, to encourage continuing growth and avoid spiritual cliques. Beginning in a small, quiet way, these prayer cells soon numbered 1500, then 3000, and now 5000 and still growing! No wonder that in Haiti, which for centuries has been a stronghold of Voodoo Satan worship, Voodoo is on the decline; and the church of Jesus Christ is increasing tremendously in spiritual power, numbers and influence."[1]

Reports come from Australia that the Baptist organization

123

of Australia is including in its programming the development of home Bible classes throughout the country. It is commonly known that the strength of the church in China and behind the Iron Curtain is the small group movement that sustains the church life.

Small Bible Study Groups in America

Here in America it is difficult to know just where and when the present growth of home Bible classes had its beginning. The church has never been without small group activity. Prayer cells and Bible studies have always been a mark of the church. However, in more recent years there has come a significant emphasis upon the small group Bible study. Some of this has been fostered by the practices of such organizations as the Navigators, Campus Crusade, Faith at Work, and other organizations which are programmed to work with small groups.

In the east, Growth by Groups and Neighborhood Bible Classes have been flourishing for some time. Women's Bible Study Fellowship, started by Miss A. Wetherell Johnson in the San Francisco area, has spread continuously from the west across the nation. Most of what we see happening to this point is taking place outside the institution of the church.

So far, only a small number of churches have really seriously developed this as part of their church life and program. But the trend is growing. The book, *Brethren, Hang Loose,* written by Robert Girard,[2] has given widespread popularity to what he is doing with small groups in his church. Recently, the Free Methodist Church has been strongly influenced by one of their pastors, Rev. Alvin Delemarter, who is promoting the home Bible class ministry, both in his denomination and with others. Over 400 pastors have taken home Bible class training in the state of Oregon and are beginning to move with it.

Many denominational leaders are expressing the hope that this Bible class program can be instituted into the churches of their denomination. The Home Missions Department of the

Evangelical Covenant Church has developed a videotape specifically to introduce the concept throughout their denomination.

A recent experiment in southern Oregon, relating to an evangelistic crusade with Luis Palau, has had some interesting results. Preceding the crusade in Grants Pass, pastors and laymen were trained to conduct home Bible classes. The classes met both preceding and during the crusade. A large number of those who responded during the crusade were channeled into these classes. It is estimated that 170 home Bible classes resulted from this program. Not only did this help to conserve the results of the crusade, but it is also having a tremendous impact on the spiritual life of the area churches.

There is every indication that this small group movement is of the Spirit for this age. It is going to grow in the future, probably with even greater rapidity than in the past. The question remains, however, will it be embraced by the church and will it become a church movement, or is it going to be an outside movement, given recognition only by a few churches.

There are many problems relating to the growth of this movement. Certainly there are many fears and misgivings in the minds of pastors. It is a movement that desperately needs dedicated leadership. That leadership, as I see it, should be from the pastors. Rather than being defensive, we need to embrace it and to give it the leadership it needs so our lay people can feel its relationship to the local church. It is my earnest hope and prayer that pastors of all denominations will embrace small group concepts for their congregations and that the movement will gain the impetus needed to affect and change our generation.

In recent times there has come a growing awareness of the person and work of the Holy Spirit among the laity. This has led to a growing interest by the body of Christ in the subject of the Holy Spirit. Though interpretations are varied and multiple concerning this subject, one thing is held in common, the gifts of the Spirit are for the edification and the building up of the church of Jesus Christ. In Paul D. Morris's book, *Love Therapy*, he makes reference to these spiritual gifts. "The Scripture teaches that each believer has one or more gifts which are to be used for self and church edification. These are to be distinguished from talent in the sense that both believers and non-believers possess certain talents. Spiritual gifts are used to communicate God's blessing and benefit to one another."[3]

Where in the present structure of the church can these spiritual gifts be properly exercised? The churches' overemphasis on monologue and inadequate emphasis on dialogue leaves much to be desired. The growth of small groups in the church will certainly give greater scope to the use of the gifts of the Spirit. I foresee in the future a healthy development in the laity of the church as they learn to use these gifts, one with another, in their homes in Bible study and prayer.

There are few who doubt that the world is in crisis. To all true believers this points only to the adequacy of God to provide what is needful for the hour. We need again the "sons of Issachar, men who understand the times" (1 Chron. 12:32, *NASB*) to keep pace with the moving of God's Spirit for our times.

It is beyond question that God is at work in the small group movements around the world. The great need in the church is to embrace this movement and give it the spiritual leadership and expertise it so sorely needs. Hopefully this flame will have been kindled in part as you have read these pages. The potential of what God can and will do through them is yet to be seen.

Footnotes

1. Quoted in a monthly newsletter published by First Baptist Church, Salem, Oregon.
2. Robert C. Girard, *Brethren, Hang Loose* (Grand Rapids: Zondervan, 1972).
3. Paul D. Morris, *Love Therapy* (Wheaton: Tyndale, 1975), p. 95.

Bibliography

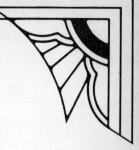

Christensen, Winnie. *Caught With My Mouth Open*. Wheaton, Il.: Harold Shaw Publishers, 1969.

Christensen, Chuck and Winnie. *God in Action*. Wheaton, Il.: Harold Shaw Publishers, 1972.

Gillquist, Peter E. *Love Is Now*. Grand Rapids: Zondervan Publishing House, 1970.

Hogue, Wilson T. *The Class Meeting*. Grand Rapids: Rose Publishing Company, 1910.

Howe, Reuel L. *The Miracle of Dialogue*. New York: Seabury Press, 1963.

Hunt, Gladys. *It's Alive*. Wheaton, Il.: Harold Shaw Publishers, 1971.

Kunz, Marilyn and Schell, Catherine. *How To Start A Bible Study*. Wheaton, Il.: Tyndale House Publishers, 1966.

Morris, Paul D. *Love Therapy*. Wheaton, Il.: Tyndale House Publishers, 1974.

Rein, Clyde. *Groups Alive-Church Alive*. New York: Harper & Row Publishers, 1969.

Smith, Jackie M. *Leading Groups in Personal Growth*. Atlanta: John Knox Press, 1973.

Williams, William. *The Experience Meeting*. Evangelical Press, 1973.

Wollen, Albert J. *How to Conduct Home Bible Classes*. Wheaton, Il.: Scripture Press Publications, Inc., 1969.